For Madelon –
And the Sounds of silence,
or – X and O in the snow –

David
Minneapolis 71

Other books by Paul Goodman

Homespun of Oatmeal Gray

Hawkweed: Poems

Five Years: Thoughts During a Useless Time

Three Plays: The Young Disciple, Faustina, Jonah

Making Do

The Lordly Hudson and Other Poems

Our Visit to Niagara

The Empire City

The Break-Up of Our Camp

Parents' Day

Stop-light and Other Noh Plays

The Facts of Life

Adam and His Works

New Reformation: Notes of a Neolithic Conservative

Like a Conquered Province: The Moral Ambiguity
of America

People or Personnel: Decentralizing and the Mixed System

Compulsory Mis-education

The Society I Live in Is Mine

The Community of Scholars

Utopian Essays and Practical Proposals

Growing Up Absurd

Drawing the Line

Communitas (*with Percival Goodman*)

Gestalt Therapy (*with F. S. Perls and Ralph Hefferline*)

Art and Social Nature

Kafka's Prayer

The Structure of Literature

Speaking
and Language:

DEFENCE
OF POETRY

Speaking and Language:

DEFENCE
OF POETRY
BY
Paul Goodman

RANDOM HOUSE   NEW YORK

ISBN: 0-394-47089-3
Library of Congress Catalog Card Number: 70-163470

Manufactured in the United States of America
by The Colonial Press, Inc., Clinton, Massachusetts

Designed by Andrew Roberts

9 8 7 6 5 4 3 2

First Edition

For my sister
Alice

Contents

Part 1

LANGUAGE

Not Speaking and Speaking

It makes a difference whether people don't speak or speak. I don't agree with the remark of Edward Sapir,

> If one says, "Lend me a dollar," I may hand it over without a word or I may give it with an accompanying "Here it is." Each of these responses is structurally equivalent if one thinks of the larger behavior pattern.

On the contrary, the immediate difference might be trivial, but the "larger behavior pattern" is likely to be different. In Sapir's example, not speaking might indicate utter simplicity of friendship, as if there were only one will between the two persons, or it might be a morose resentment at being tapped and not accepting the other as exactly a person; but speaking would recognize him as a person.

Consider the difference between the fellow who snaps his fingers at his companion and leaves, expecting the other to follow like a dog, and the one who says "Let's go," however curtly. When spoken to, one is included at least as a human being. Yet a friend might get up and leave without a word or with a glance (but not snapping his fingers), and his friend follows him because they are totally in accord. This is like the silent agreement that is reached in a primitive tribal council that baffles the anthropologist because he did not hear any vote or decision.

Speaking is a commitment not only to a human relationship with the one spoken to, but also, we shall see, to the existence of the thing spoken about. A common ploy of resentment is to refuse to speak, to force the other to the humiliation of admitting that he needs the relationship by speaking first. A jealous man may not talk about the question of fact that he suspects, either because he will not admit the possible existence of the fact or he will not admit that he cares about it. A solitary man—every man in his solitude—has no one to talk to. Yet very close friends often do not speak, because they do not have to.

Thus, there is a silence that is preverbal, not yet interpersonal or even personal. There is speaking, which recognizes persons. And there is a silence beyond speech, an accord closer than verbal communication and where the situation is unproblematic. In one of the scriptural lives of Buddha there is a remarkable sentence, at the conversion of Anathapindika: "The Lord consented by becoming silent." I take it that this means that the silence of the Lord creates accord, *is* accord; and from the human point of view, if the *Lord* consents, what further is to be said?

More generally, I am unhappy with the fundamental linguistic formula of Leonard Bloomfield. He divides an incident of speech into three parts: (A) practical events preceding the act of speech; (B) speech; (C) practical events following the act of speech. And he says,

When anything apparently unimportant turns out to be closely connected with more important things, we say that it has, after all, a "meaning"; it "means" these more important things. Accordingly, we say that speech-utterance, trivial and unimportant in itself, is important because it has a *meaning:* the meaning consists of the important things with which the speech-utterance (B) is connected, namely the practical events (A and C).

No; speech adds meaning to the events. Sometimes it is their most important meaning. Very often it is, by its form and expressiveness, the fulfillment of the preceding practical events and the shaper of the succeeding events. It is itself a practical event.

The speechlessness of mystics seems sometimes to come from a preverbal physical or biological confluence with the environment; they are in a trance, "rolled round in earth's diurnal course," as Wordsworth says, "with rocks and stones and trees." But sometimes mystical silence seems to indicate a fullness of meaning beyond the ability or need of saying, as in *Wachet Auf* Bach sings of the marriage with Jesus: "No ear has ever heard such joy."

We can give more mundane examples. John Dewey points out that to many people "It is repellant or artificial to speak of *any* consummatory event." Such an event is to be enjoyed, or mourned, in itself, though one might speak of its on-going consequences. We say of a beautiful scene, a sunset, that "it speaks for itself," meaning that it doesn't speak and neither need we. When Dewey remarried at seventy, a reporter asked him to pick out a passage about marriage from one of his books. Surprised, the author of so many books on morals, education, and society, confessed that he had never written about marriage. It is the testimony of a well-balanced and happy man—especially a pragmatist. When there's no problem, there's nothing to say. There are countless novels about courtship or adultery, almost none about happy marriage.

Yet there is a contrary truth that limits this one. It is precisely consummatory experience, whether joy or grief, that we finite creatures often cannot contain. We are made anxious by too much excitement or even feel that we are going mad, and then our human way of coping with our feelings is to say them, for example in poems of praise or lamentation. These cases too are countless. People return from a trip abroad and are too full of it, so they have to blab about it in order to get back to ordinary life. A man is in love and has to blab about it to get us involved as accomplices in his way-out condition. Such people are boring or embarrassing because so much talk doesn't seem to be called for. Another man, a writer, loses his son and writes repetitious poems of his grief; since writing is his way of being in the world, he has no other way of coming back.

A powerful principle of recent higher criticism of the Bible, in both Martin Buber and Karl Barth, is grounded in this human disposition. Events occurred that were stupefying, catastrophically confusing; to preserve their sanity, people confabulated the Bible stories. *Something* occurred, but not what is written down.

> From such texts [says Buber], we cannot arrive at "what really happened" . . . but we can recover much of how people experienced the events. With such texts it is wrong to talk of historization of myth [as the early Higher Criticism did], rather they are mythization of history.

In my opinion, however, *all* spoken sentences assert, indicate belief in, the existence of the state of affairs that they say, or they *mean* to be lies and thereby also tailor the world to the forms and conditions of speech. Of course, an immense amount of palaver is not meant to mean much of anything, for instance the small talk that is used for social cement—I think I remember an actual count that small talk was more than 95 percent of sentences spoken; even so, small talk is not permitted to be nonsense or *mere* sentence forms, though it must not be taken too literally. When people seriously join subjects and predicates, they mean to be making propositions, not just propositional skeletons. When people make interjections, of surprise or woe, they are not singing; they mean to be saying how it is with themselves. Poetic fictions are always statements, though not in propositional sentences.

In recent linguistic theory, this has tended to be denied by formalist and positivist linguists, who want to discuss only sentence structures and what they call "language events." They define language as the simplest constructible or describable framework of language behavior. Utterances are utterances, period. They can define how they want, but we must ask what the speakers and hearers of language are *doing,* because this will influence the forms. The linguists deny this too—that meanings influence forms, but I will show otherwise. A correct grammar of a natural language like English cannot be constructed apart from its being spoken and taking the meanings into account.

I am more convinced by the example given by John Austin. If a man says, "The cat is on the mat, but I don't believe it," we turn away in disgust because he is insincere, he is trifling with us. The fact that the listener does this, that he will not dignify the noise as language, is certainly crucial in the language event. Immanuel Kant put it strictly: There is a categorical imperative to tell the truth, for if the possibility of not meaning what one says is universalized, there is a self-contradiction in the nature of speech, and human speech is impossible. When a man is known for a liar, there is less speech altogether.

Thus, if somebody doubts that we mean what we are saying, we often employ the dumb-bunny expedient of just saying it louder—we *say* it more. Here is an important example in the grammar of English. "Be" has a tendency to become a mere connective—a copula—to state identities, to link subjects and adjectives, to include a class in a bigger class, as "This is John," "He's lazy," "Men are mammals." But consider the common sequence, "You're lazy. I'm not lazy. You *are* lazy!" Here, under stress of contradiction, the existential force of the copula leaps right back to the surface when we say it louder; "be" now does not merely take a predicate, it is itself a predicate, a verb: "Laziness inheres in you by nature ('be' from a verb like φύω)—you're just like your father." [1] Analogously, "I *did* see him," "I *will* go, no matter what you say"—emphasized, the formal auxiliary recovers its lexical meaning. (Incidentally, in such cases is the emphasis a phoneme or a morpheme, lexical or semantic?)

My hunch is that when "be" really becomes otiose in English, when it does not add anything, it will be dropped, as often in Latin. Thus, in Black English, which is economical, "you lazy" is quite correct. But the black speaker, too, will say, "you *are* lazy."

Because speaking *is* assertive, it holds the floor, it com-

---

1. Noam Chomsky certainly overstates the case when he says that "be" never states existence:

> In the simplest grammar of English, there is never any reason to incorporate "be" into the class of verbs . . . rather than "be + Predicate."

Let us review some cases. "I think, therefore I am" is fancy and probably not English. Shakespere's "to be or not to be, that is the question" and "I cannot but remember such things were" are certainly English, but they are poetical. "Let there be light! and there was light"—here both parts are good prose, meaningful to most people, but the case is special. "Let the child be," meaning "leave him alone as he is," is not special. On the basis of these, we come directly to: "You *are* lazy"—the existential force was there all along.

mands authority, whereas keeping still is retiring and modest, or at least biding its time. Children should be seen and not heard because—we have decided—they don't know anything to assert. In a parliamentary filibuster, a speaker's right to continue is respected just because he is speaking; by a legal fiction he is asserting something, even if he is asserting nothing. If he were only making noise or doing tricks, or if he somehow made it clear that he was using language as sentence forms, would he then be out of order? I don't think this constitutional nicety has ever been tested by the Court.

The only common sentences that are not assertive are tautologies, where predicates rather obviously repeat what is in the subjects; and such sentences, when the tautology is exposed, are met with ridicule or boredom, or it is agreed that they be stricken from the discourse as if they had not been said. Recent linguistics, however, has been modeling itself on positivist symbolic logic, which claims to be nothing but strings of tautologies, "analytic sentences," and this logic in turn has modeled itself on algebra that indeed gets its force by exhibiting identities. In my opinion, the idea of common speech is much more like the theory of logic of the older British logicians, e.g. F. H. Bradley and Bernard Bosanquet, who held that the subject of all predication is ultimately the nature of things, Reality, which they liked to write with a big capital letter:

$$R^a_b$$

—that is, the nature of things is such that when viewed as a it is b.

As I shall try to show later, poetry is also assertive, but it does not say sentences and sometimes does not use words of the common code. Rather, since assertion is ultimately assertion of reality, poetry tries to go about the business more directly, by tying down more reality in its complicated structures than is possible in ordinary sentences and by trying to make the poem itself like a real thing. (See Chapter VIII.)

A poignant corollary of the assertiveness of speech is the speech-embarrassment of alienated young people who feel that they have no world to assert, and therefore they pepper every sentence with "like" or "you know?" meaning that, though they are speaking, they do not mean to be saying precisely what they are saying and the world is not theirs to say.

However, if speaking, especially speaking seriously, means to assert a state of affairs, then, if one has a morals or metaphysics of non-attachment, skepticism, *maya,* transcendentalism, or illimitable unity, there is something inauthentic in talking much about it, especially in prose sentences. A long apologetic for Zen Buddhism doesn't make sense; the more the philosophy is talked, the less believable it becomes. The appropriate behavior is not to speak, or at most to make an occasional puzzling or derisive remark, or to tell an anecdote like a Zen *koan* or an Hasidic parable, whose meaning is in the listener's silent interpretation and perhaps enlightenment. Wittgenstein said this succinctly, "What you can't talk about, you must hush up about." Lao-tzu said, "The Way that can be told is not an unvarying way . . . therefore the Sage carries on wordless teaching." (It's not fair to taunt him with inconsistency for making a book of 5,000 words, as Po Chu-I does; that's a skimpy output for such an old sage, and compiled by his disciples at that.) Confucius did not mention spiritual beings, though he probably believed in them. Plato would not lecture on the Idea of the Good. Medieval Jewish scholars forbade talking metaphysics except to the one chosen disciple. The alchemists were equally hermetic. In these traditions, speaking as such implies intervention, presumptuous assertiveness, definition, cutting the world down to size, vulgarizing, blasphemy, black magic. Speaking is regarded as itself a proposition.

Similarly, for those who have a nihilistic goal, to bring down the established order by deeds, it does not pay to sound off about their intentions. Jacob Frank the Sabbatian said, "Just as a man who wishes to conquer a fortress does not do it by making a speech but must go there himself with all his forces, so we must go our own way in silence." But note that he did say it, publishing a manifesto from the underground. For human beings there is evidently something more important than to win; they must explain themselves and have company. James Joyce prescribed "Silence, cunning, exile," but he wrote, and some of it made him trouble.

Classical Japanese drama, Noh, is remarkable in having an elaborated convention of what is spoken, and with what genres of speech, and what is not spoken. Entrance marches and introducing the action are descriptive and discursive speech. Meeting with the protagonist still unrevealed in his true nature is dialogue. The revelation is lyric poetry. The climactic dance is wordless. The climax of the dance is not even danced. The envoi includes scriptural quotations. A Noh play imitates coming to awareness, and in this process some moments require speaking for their realization, others require silence.

Music can accompany, heighten, and realize both speaking and silence. It is sometimes like one, sometimes like the other, and sometimes like neither. When I walk through a meadow or an interesting museum and begin to hum a tune, as I do, is this music the preverbal expression of animal satisfaction, as children sing after supper or as insects hum when the sun comes from behind a cloud, or is it a cognitive formulation more subtle than words? It is striking that, though I am a writer, I do *not* think of verses of a poem, though I may do so later, in other circumstances, recollecting the incident in tranquillity.

There are opposite pathologies: speaking when not speaking is called for, and keeping mum when speech is called for. Both kinds are unfortunately common. For instance, the correct conclusion of a practical syllogism is not a third proposition but doing something. If a man says he wants something and it is made available, the conclusion is to take it and not talk about taking it. When something ought to be done and there are means to do it, it is suspicious if people do not do it but go on discussing it. If people blab on in such cases, they mean to prevent action and to exhaust in words the feelings that motivate to action. With a neurotic, this might indicate ambivalence about the original wish; he does not really want what he said he wanted. With administrators and statesmen it is a common kind of fraud; they appoint committees of experts to study what has already been well studied, and then they disregard the findings anyway.

> "It is a weakness in Shakespere that his people blab away *in extremis,* granting that it is sometimes splendid blabbing. One is almost reminded of the hilarious scene in *Medea* when, within, she is killing the screaming children and the Chorus outside keeps chattering, 'Oh dear, something is amiss.' " [Preface to *Three Plays*]

On the other hand, there is the fellow who falls speechless and keeps you hanging. Forty thousand years elapse while he characteristically grinds his molars. What's going on, from his point of view, is that he's "thinking," perhaps carrying on an interior monologue in which he offers to himself various formulations and rejects them. Sometimes in this state of absorption, he imagines that he has been speaking out. Effectually, he excludes you, but he holds you fast, waiting. You get exasperated, which may be his intention.

Normally—though there are exceptions—people do not "think" before they speak, as if speech were a translation of prior thoughts rather than a part of the process of thought, or as if it were a description or consequence of feeling rather than an organic part of feeling. Normally one just speaks and makes sense as he goes along. Memory, perception, syllogism, style and tone that are feelingful and adjust to the listener, these are in the spoken words themselves, by habit, somewhat by instinct, and continually shaped and invented in each present situation. Speaking is one way of taking and making a present situation. When a person "thinks" before he speaks, watches what he says, censors before he says, he may be afraid of sounding stupid or crazy, he may be suspicious and afraid of being trapped, he may be embarrassed because he is repressing exhibition or hostility. He may have a conceited image of himself as if his words were *ex cathedra,* so he has to pay them out. There are indeed situations in life that are so problematic or portentous that it is hard to find words or it is necessary to weigh one's words; but they are rare. Most often the flow of speech in dialogue is itself the best method of exploring the subject and discovering the right words. In my observation, too much going to school and being quizzed inhibits people from speaking naturally; instead of saying what they have to say, they have to figure out beforehand what the teacher wants them to say. For learning to write (and read), school-going is a disaster.

Since we pretty reliably know the occasions for not speaking and for speaking, silence gives information, sometimes crashingly. A child tests out an adult, raising the ante; the silence—and the thickness of the silence—tells him, sometimes quite precisely, what the limits are. An unanswered letter usually speaks more forcefully than an answer. When the chiefs of the Great Powers do *not* talk over the hot-line, we learn that the current international crisis is not quite worth destroying mankind for. In such cases, however, silence does not seem to be as assertive, as committal, as speech. In passional personal situations, we nag the other to say it out, whether "I love you" or "I can't stand you." In sessions of group therapy, people cannot stand long silence; sometimes they explain that it makes them feel naked, revealed. Perhaps the information given by not speaking has in it too much potentiality and possible surprise; it requires great confidence to endure it. In general, not speaking seems to give a broader, more contextual, kind of information, whereas spoken sentences give more pointed foreground information.

Nevertheless, there is one major kind of not speaking, namely listening, that is at least as pointed and precise as speech and that continually forces speakers to refine their speech in the minutest detail, to give the drift, to avoid ambiguity, to focus attention. The active silence of listening determines the phonetics, the lexicon, the grammar, and the style of speaking. The sharpest contemporary linguists say that what is heard, rather than what is said, is the most accurate basis for the study of language—e.g., C. J. Bailey, a disciple of William Labov: "Hearing and production are not symmetrical. Understanding of sounds is closer to competence than production of sounds is." Naturally, as a writer, I think that there is a special virtue in creative production, but the language of a writer is always tempered to be "as clear as possible"; he has in mind an "ideal audience"—that is, silent indeed, most being dead. The same tension obtains in good colloquial speech between being as expressive as possible and being as clear as possible. In my opinion, it is this tension—rather than common code or symmetry between production and hearing—that is the essence of the study of language. (Needless to say, I take linguistics as one of the humanities, esthetic and political. It cannot be "value-free" any more than any other of the behavioral sciences.)

Thus, not speaking and speaking are both human ways of being in the world, and there are kinds and grades of each. There is the dumb silence of slumber or apathy; the sober silence that goes with a solemn animal face; the fertile silence of awareness, pasturing the soul, whence emerge new thoughts; the alive silence of alert perception, ready to say, "This . . . this . . ."; the musical silence that accompanies absorbed activity; the silence of listening to another speak, catching the drift and helping him be clear; the noisy silence of resentment and self-recrimination, loud with subvocal speech but sullen to say it; baffled silence; the silence of peaceful accord with other persons or communion with the cosmos.

There is the speech that names things and reads off sentences of how they are; that defines an essence and reasons from it; that creates and maintains community bonds; that recognizes the other as a person, asks questions, and exchanges information; that directly touches another by imperatives; that exteriorizes and shares what one is feeling. There is the speech of the literary process that travels a thesis from the beginning to the middle to the end, and the poetic speech that alleviates an inner problem by bringing it into the public forum and then reconstructs the world in words.

The uses of not speaking and speaking are quite specific, and my hunch is that they are quite exclusive. Perhaps some cases overlap, when either behavior is appropriate, but I cannot think of important examples. That what must be shown cannot be said is more than a tautology. For instance, an anatomical demonstration of a corpse is not an illustration of the lecture but a way of teaching in its own right that makes the lecture make sense; starting from that sense, the lecture, too, has its own kind of message. Sensations are not describable. Some feelings are not even nameable. Sometimes music says them more accurately than speech can. Esthetic criticism depends on the prior enjoyment of artworks that are criticized; the verbal criticism is no substitute, yet it is a valuable experience in its own right. And a long line of philosophers has held that the unity or individuality of anything, though it is intellectually knowable, cannot be said in propositions; yet it is the beginning of all judgments and science. (This is the main theme of Kant's *Critique of Judgment*.)

On the other hand, except in trivial cases, there is never an adequate non-verbal substitute for words. Speech is not just one of a number of our instruments for defining experience, realizing ourselves, and communicating with one another, but occupies a special place. In theory, behaviorist psychologists would like to do without verbal reports, but they finally always include speaking and the meaning of the speech as an essential part of human behavior. In his late *Logic,* John Dewey undertook to construct a theory of enquiry based entirely on the operations in laboratories, but when he came to structure them he found, to his surprise, that the result was very like the old logic based on sentences. It is a current mania among people in "multi-media" to say that literature is *passé* and even speaking is on its way out, but non-verbal media cannot convey a definition, syllogism, period, exposition, metaphor, or narration. And I'll bet that people will go on talking.

For human beings silence and speaking are complementary and are best understood together, as limits of each other or contrasted, as I have been contrasting them. They both seem to be primordial conditions from birth—there is no real "infancy," and it is as easy to conceive of mankind emerging from chattering monkeys as of our ancestors first breaking the silence with speech. The need—or choice—not to speak or to speak is one of the most interesting things about us.

I think Bloomfield is wrong when he says, "The situations which prompt people to utter speech include every object and happening in their universe." Some happenings cannot prompt speech, and some speech creates a situation in the universe rather than being prompted by one. It is often good advice to shut up and not start something. And I do not agree with those phenomenologists, e.g. Maurice Merleau-Ponty, who say that all intention wants to complete itself in saying. Meaning does want to exteriorize itself, for animals live *in* their environments and are unthinkable apart from them; but the completion of an intention can often occur without talking. I think that Malinowski, as a communitarian, overstates the case when he speaks of the necessity of talking because of "the imperative of establishing ties of social communion." To be social-cement *is* perhaps the chief use of speech; but community is natural, and it does not need to be established. If somebody were twisting my arm for an answer, I would guess that community makes speech possible rather than that speech establishes community.

Consider this case: a man attentively repairing his automobile engine checks the fuel pump and carburetor, decides that the trouble must be in the spark, cleans the points, and finally notices and repairs a broken wire—all this without a word, external or internal. It is pointless to say that he is subvocally murmuring the names of the parts as he proceeds; he's humming a tune, and what he seems to be doing, at least, is feeling himself into the operation of the engine. Meantime, his friend is going along with him in the same wordless behavior, attentively following the procedure and handing him the appropriate tools. And the completion of this highly intentional and highly communal behavior occurs when the driver turns the key, the car starts, and they both smile. At *this* point, of consummation, they are almost sure to say something, if only "Oof!"

On the other hand, the fact that somebody speaks is not always a big deal, an intervention, the creation of a new situation, a consummation, an "excess of our existence over nature," as Merleau-Ponty puts it. Speaking may often be just a routine continuance of nature. Some people never shut up, just as I never stop writing. We say, dramatically, that we break the silence, as if the silence were there primordially; but maybe it was never quiet. The clamor of a cocktail party in a room sounds very much like the clamor in a tropical forest, and there is perhaps neither more nor less communication (or poetry) going on. It is a talkative and sociable species, and when people are together it is usually uneasy if they do *not* talk—Malinowski speaks of "the strange and unpleasant tension which men feel when facing each other in silence." Much of being alone and almost all of what is called "thinking" are subvocal talk. We must often exert a strong act of will to break off talking and let the silence flood back. Some monastic orders impose on the monks a rule of periodic not talking, because the world is too much with us.

CHAPTER II

Speaking as an Action, Speech as a Thing

When speaking intervenes in the world and shapes experience, it often is, or is taken as, a direct action in the environment, an energy or even a physical thing, rather than the use of the common code for communication. We can show a wide range of important cases where this is so; one cannot understand what language is without taking it into account.

The scientific linguists of the past couple of generations are here curiously inconsistent. They want to be entirely "objective," to start from the data just as they are; yet on this subject, they brush aside the data. To quote Bloomfield:

> Popular belief, the world over, exaggerates the effect of language in superstitious ways (magic formulae, charms, curses name-tabu, and the like), but at the same time takes no account of its obvious and normal effects.

Disregarding popular belief and use, the linguists lay all their stress on the instrumental function of speech—language is the "means of communication and expression" (Sapir); speech sounds essentially are "signals" (Bloomfield). In fact, they usually have little to say about "expression" either, except that it is terribly prevalent. It does not seem to me to be objective to discuss language and leave out some of its chief uses, which are also "obvious and normal."

A baby bawling rather directly compels his mother's response. The bawling is, of course, what the ancients called a natural sign, a physical rather than conventional consequence of his physical malaise, as smoke is a sign of fire. It is possible that the mother's attention is also biologically compelled—I have read somewhere that a doe responds to her baby when she has undergone labor, but not when she has given birth under anesthesia. In any case, infant and mother exist in an organic unity simpler than the deliberate purposes of either, e.g. suckling is necessary for both. And this seems obvious when a woman wakes from apparently sound sleep at her own baby's whimper.

An infant bawling is not speaking; the act is prior to the formation of his verbal ego or his learning the language. Yet it would be strange if some such physical bond did not continue to underlie the small talk and chatter which constitute most of conversation as a social glue. People chatter when they are together, and this glues them together, even when they do not exchange information. The taciturnity of New England farmers, well-bred persons, and Noble Savages is almost surely a social pathology.

Older books always used to print imperatives as exclamations—not only "Watch out!" but "Give it to me!"—because we often say them with more force than the surrounding words. There is a kind of physical action at a distance in them, pushing, tugging, touching, pointing. Correspondingly, we say them not merely as code to be understood but as if we hope they'll be heard with an immediate reflexive response. My feeling for English is that it is highly unlikely that "Watch out!" has a "You" to be understood as the subject of the verb, as traditional grammars have asserted, and, again, Chomsky in trying to construct the "simplest grammar." It is less artificial to take the absence of the subject at face value and say that imperatives never were sentences talking about the world, but were direct actions.

A linguistic consequence of the direct action in the imperatives is that they have become sparser in "middle class" speech than in aristocratic or common speech. For both better and worse, "middle class" people are self-conscious, squeamish, chary about being pushed around or pushing people around; their speech becomes peppered with I's, indirect constructions, avoidance of commands.[1]

The case of the imperatives is interesting because philosophers of language like Buber proceed in exactly the opposite direction from traditional grammar and scientific linguistics, and suggest that combining subjects and predicates, the whole of propositional speech, originated in the imperatives and other kinds of direct address in I-Thou dialogue. Thus it would be only later, in the third person, when we introduce things talked about, that we need to add subjects to imperatives: "Long live the King!" *"Fiat*

1. B. F. Skinner maintains the general thesis that speech is absolutely conditioned and trained by the hearers (grownups), who use it for control. I don't think this is too useful for explaining most sentences (most meaning is far more complicated); but just in the case of what Skinner calls "mands"—commands, requests, questions —there may be something in it. A cold response to such a "mand"— a person who objects to being "shouted at," an adult who pays no attention to a child's question—can quickly change the style of the speaker.

lux." But this too seems to me to be wrong-headed. *Prima facie,* men perceive and know about, and do, and do things together cooperatively, and *prima facie,* all languages are apt for objective communication about the world and are used instrumentally. The grammar of a language will be found by taking into account the many uses of speaking the language.

The bluntest use of speech as a physical thing is obstructive and disruptive shouts and chanting for political purposes. Of course it need not be speech—any noises will do. This use is close to the football and war yells of juvenile gangs and primitives, creating solidarity in the group and disheartening the enemy. Unfriendly critics would say that it is even closer to infantile bawling and tantrums, and I myself have written about students at Berkeley, "They do not sound like Isaac Newton, more a mob of monkeys." Yet the use of noisy speech as a physical thing, to disrupt routine and compel attention, is politically rational for any group that believes it is constitutionally powerless and therefore has recourse to the irreducible political power that everybody has, his bodily behavior in the space that he occupies, which others have to cope with if they are nearby.

During the troubles of the thirties, political agitators were told to scream if they were arrested, to attract public notice. And those who want to take over an organization by parliamentary means see to it that their spokesmen in the audience get up one after another and never let the opposition get a word in edgewise.

Turn now to some rubrics of ancient and modern law. In the nature of the case, law is naively realistic and deals in physical actions and things, not searching much into intentions, and disregarding meanings altogether. This guarantees that it will be stupider than sociology or psychology, and quite unfit to regulate human intercourse, but it makes it a better source for anthropology.

Blasphemy is speech that by its very utterance offends the gods and puts the tribe in jeopardy. *Lèse majesté* is speech or symbolic action that in itself offends the King. Thus, Shakespere had to excise the deposition scene from *Richard II* because it was bad news that kings were deposed. Recently the United States Congress made it a felony to burn a draft card, not because this action in any way helped a youth evade the draft but because it insulted the dignity of the State. Obscenity is speech or behavior that by its very doing violates a taboo and causes social shock; it is not necessary to produce in court anybody who has been shocked. Crazy speech is likely to lead to involuntary commitment, not because it is harmful to the disturbed person or anybody else but because it rouses general anxiety. Certain themes, for instance the subject of *Stavrogin's Confession* or *Lolita,* are unmentionable as such; their publication in a book is tantamount to calling the forbidden behavior into being.

Pornography seems to be assessed rather by hearing the speech than speaking it; it is a physical cause of something evil in the hearer—sexual activity, more specifically masturbation. Fighting words may not be said because they directly lead to trouble from the hearer. Here there is something more like communication.

In all these cases, it is the existence or direct effect of words that is guilty. For the information communicated there is constitutional freedom of speech; one may talk *about* the themes or concepts. This paradox has led Judge Frank to comment that, if an idea is eloquently presented, it is in danger of prosecution; if it is dully presented, it is safe.

In some recent indictments for conspiracy in the United States, it is not clear—I doubt that it ever *can* be clear—how much the conspirators were planning a dangerous action and how much they were just sounding off out of frustration. In the cases of some of the black militants, however, I suspect that they were indicted largely because their speech pattern is violent by white standards.

But the Law tells us not only about active words that misbehave, but also about creative words that call beneficent institutions into being, that found institutions and remain with them like indispensable fixed things, like the foundations of a building. Indeed, a large part of law consists of the direct action of right words, legal procedure; and it must be so to establish jurisdiction, the rules to be followed in the trial, the relevance of the statutes. If the proper person says, "I dub thee knight," you *are* a knight, and if the Queen calls you an hereditary peer, your children also will be peers. A minister *pronounces* a couple man and wife; without his pronouncement their souls might be damned and their children's inheritance be in jeopardy. By the authority vested in him by the States of New York, Pennsylvania, or others, by words alone the Chancellor of the University creates a Doctor of Philosophy; and this case is especially remarkable, since, by a compromise on investiture reached in the thirteenth century in Paris, he *must* elevate the candidate chosen by the Faculty and presented by its Dean, so in fact he decides and does nothing. Yet his creative words make a big difference to a man's career and salary.

The operative part of a legal document consists in writing and signing some words, e.g. "I make him my heir." In equity, a written and signed contract has a good chance of binding future behavior. A dollar bill is legal tender for all debts, public and private, because it says so over the signature of the Secretary of the Treasury, provided the bill is not counterfeit and was printed on the right paper in the right place.

There is a permanent substantiality in certain texts that goes far beyond their original purpose to communicate. The Declaration of Independence is preserved under glass not merely as a memento but as if we would not be independent of England without its existence. In an important sense, the French Revolution consisted in burning up such pieces of parchment. Commentators, apologists, and jurists "save" the texts of Scripture and the Constitution much as physical scientists "save" the phenomena; new beliefs must be formulated and new conditions must be coped with so as not to contradict the texts. In mandarin societies like ours, blue books have a determining effect on licensing and hiring, though the evidence is overwhelming that such verbal exercises are irrelevant to performance on the job. And just as hard-hats are outraged if anybody burns an American flag, I am outraged if anybody burns a book, no matter what, including *Mein Kampf*.

God created the world from nothing with words. A prophet's lips touched with a coal of fire create new ethics. If an ordained priest says *"Hoc est Corpus,"* the wheaten bread is transfigured. A man can win salvation by repeating the one right syllable, or even spinning it on a wheel.

Obviously such beliefs in the amazing energy that resides in speech are continuous with, often identical with, the ancient verbal magic of spells and curses, and it is hard to collect them without finally becoming sarcastic and tired of humanity. Yet they are not an abuse of language, but an essential part of the power of language. The belief in verbal magic is not a trivial error that can be outgrown. Despite General Semantics, we—like, no doubt, our primitive forefathers—do know the difference between a name and a thing and that the map is not the territory. Children know the difference and believe in verbal magic anyway. Verbal magic is not like the simple magic by contiguity that Sir James G. Frazer talked about, which could be methodically corrected by more accurate observation and science. In Chapter V, I will collect some linguistic reasons why there comes to exist a verbalized world, even a verbal world, as an autonomous entity. Here let me offer some background considerations.

Institutions are grounded in lasting social solidarity, and ritual words are one of the strongest glues that maintain solidarity. Rarely do communities or institutions survive by rational function, though they must also function to survive. So the words must be more than rational instruments. And one of the most powerful institutions is the conventional language itself. It is very close to the ideology, and it shapes how people think, feel, and judge what *is* functional. Thus verbal magic tends to be self-proving: We judge what works largely according to how we are and what we therefore believe, and how we are largely depends on our language. We look with a critical eye at systems of ideology, verbal magic, and false religion—it is harder to do in the present than in the past, but there is no example of a society without such a system.

Besides, taken uncritically, as people take them, words do work physical magic: The nature of things is amenable to being manipulated by words, spectacularly in science and technology. Powerful sentences like the inverse square law of gravity and $E = mc^2$ are sentences. Critical philosophies like pragmatism and operationalism have tried to de-verbalize science and reduce its explanations to efficient causes, non-verbal behavior, and the manipulation of things. But people ask what the laboratory operations or the behaviors "mean"; they want a fuller kind of explanation and they are not satisfied with the answer "Nothing," which is obviously a hoax, for nothing comes from nothing. Another critical approach tries to take the metaphysics out of language by devising methodical languages which are just "postulated." But, unfortunately, directions for the use of a tight methodical language have to be said in everyday language, and ambiguity and magic seep back.[2] And even more important, that a formal language can be applied to real things seems to most people (and to me, too) to be exactly magic. If mathematics is just an agreed-on procedure, it is sheer magic that it works so well. Meantime, scientists themselves, not to speak of the rest of us, persist in using the language that suits them. To de-mystify words is not a novel idea; it goes from Socrates and Hsün-tze to Rudolf Carnap and Otto Neurath. The only methodical language that seems to catch on internationally and across the boundaries of disciplines is computer language, and this has been for technological and commercial reasons, not prophylaxis. (In my opinion, it is not an adequate language; cf. *New Reformation,* pp. 16–17, quoted below, pp. 130-31, footnote 5.)

Anyway, a belief in efficacious magic of some kind is inevitable for a species like man that lives by creativity, by adapting its environment to itself. The environment is various and precarious, and, to survive, a man must feel that he can change it to his advantage by willing—though, of course, it would often be to his advantage to will and create a good deal less. In *Gestalt Therapy,* I define normal psychology as the study of creative adjustments, distinguishing it from neurosis—interrupted creativity. But indeed, a lot of creativity seems to be quite gratuitous, not adjustive at all, and there is no rule by which to know beforehand. People are everywhere busy-busy thinking up new ways to play or make trouble. Man believes himself not omnipotent but indefinitely potent until he meets recalcitrant facts that he must compound with, with the prudence that luckily

2. E.g. Carnap, in introducing a symbolic convention, definition, or rule of inference: " 'A' will be used to represent the class '---'. Let A . . . then. . . ." What is the meaning of "represent" or "let"?

is also natural to him. And speaking, which pours out so spontaneously relevant in so many circumstances, is an archetype of human plastic power. Among its powers is to label things and then to manipulate the labels—referring back to reality, manufacturing a mixture.

Poets and writers of fiction have rarely regarded their poetic speech as communication of information in the common code, and certainly not as "self-expression," but usually as a physical thing, a direct action on the audience or a free act in the void. In classical literary theory, poems are imitations; and the discussion of imitations is either how to make them "like whole animals," as Aristotle puts it, self-subsistent and internally coherent; or, as Plato puts it in *Ion,* imitations come from the energy flowing directly from divine ideas, through the mesmerized poet, into copies that are as real as any other creatures. (In *The Republic,* where they are only third-rate copies, there are no poets.) In these views there is a kind of fetishism, as if speaking and communication were in the words themselves, apart from any human speaker: "The very language," says Merleau-Ponty, "itself teaches itself and carries its meaning to the listener. A piece of music, at first not understood, finally creates its own public if indeed it *says* something." But this fetishism is somewhat valid; speech does form people.

In Renaissance criticism, going back to Horace, poems are said to instruct and delight. However, this is hardly ever taken to mean that they pleasantly communicate a message or communicate a pleasant message, but rather that, by enticing and moving the listener, a poem engages him in its peculiar kind of truth-telling. For instance, in high Italian theory, it is *only* eloquence, the moving statement and the moved response, that tells the truth; merely scientific sentences are not true, because nothing humanly important follows from them. And in Dryden's mature criticism, finally, this gets to mean that poetry instructs *by* moving, by shaking the listener out of his routine responses. Norbert Wiener, the father of cybernetics, has beautifully restated Dryden's idea by saying that a poet—his example is Keats—conveys more information than a scientific reporter, because he deranges the code rather than simply applies the common code to new material. Consider the scientific revolution initiated by Einstein by changing a couple of basic words of the code.

Since the Romantic period, most modern theory has dealt with the peculiar act of the poet rather than his product or its effect on the audience; but the thrust has been the same. The poet must "say the thing," not "talk about it" or "communicate his thoughts." For Wordsworth, the poet's speech, which comes to him in tranquil recollection of an event, is the same as the essence of the event. In Cubist theory, best explained by the painter Cézanne, the artist does not copy the world in his medium but reconstructs it according to his medium (this was also Aristotle's doctrine). Gide advises the young poet to follow his rimes and not his thoughts, and then his poem will come out real. Genet says that he knows what ethical value to put on persons and actions by how well he can write them.

The most extreme assertions that speech is a physical action occur in the essays of Antonin Artaud, collected in *The Theater and Its Double,* which have been the manifestos of contemporary revolutionary theater. Artaud is more interested in affecting the audience than the previous critics; he is less artistic, but what he wants to communicate is not meanings. Right language is the power "not to define thoughts but to *cause thinking,*" "to make use of [speech] in a concrete and spatial sense . . . to manipulate it like a solid object, one which overturns and disturbs things, in the air first of all." "Sounds, noises, cries are chosen first of all for their vibratory quality." "I propose to bring back into the theater this elementary magical idea, taken up by modern psychoanalysis, which consists in effecting a patient's cure by making him assume the apparent and exterior attitudes of the desired condition." The "painful cleavage" of culture from life "is responsible for the revenge of *things;* the poetry which is no longer within us and which we no longer succeed in finding in things suddenly appears on their wrong side: consider the unprecedented number of crimes whose perverse gratuitousness is explained only by our powerlessness to take complete possession of life." "The old totemism of animals, stones, objects capable of discharging thunderbolts is dead for us." "To make metaphysics out of a spoken language is to use it in a new, exceptional, and unaccustomed fashion, to reveal its possibilities for producing physical shock." Naturally, his model is the Balinese dance, where the dancers lose the sense that it is theater, physically attack one another, sink into trance.

There is some paranoia in these remarks; he has blinders on—speech is not so simple. The theater of cruelty does not work; using words as brickbats is pretty soon a crashing bore. The audience resists being pushed around so easily; only the speaker himself is moved. (I have observed the same with poems written under the influence of drugs: only the poet who was drugged knows how super-real the images are; the audience finds them about as thrilling as the Revelation of John of Patmos.) Like most paranoia, however, it contains an important truth: The essence of theater is not a well-wrought play, and it is certainly not a message. It is *coup de théâtre.* But the *coup* must be subtilely prepared through modification of the common words and the plotted but surprising entrance—as by Racine.

Let me end these first remarks about poetry by going

back to points of law. To the extent that poems and fictions are things or direct actions, as poets claim, they do not qualify for the guarantee of free speech as a civil liberty. Freedom of speech has meant that authority may not interfere with political persuasion, stump-speaking, editorializing, pamphleteering, and there is to be no felony of seditious libel of the State or public officers. The speech of art is force; it is not democratic persuasion. I don't think that closing the theaters was thought to be a violation of civil liberty. And Magistrate Mead could plausibly say, about paintings of D. H. Lawrence, "Obscene pictures should be put an end to like any wild animal that may be dangerous."

But therefore we writers are all the more passionate in our claim to absolute freedom of speech, and we rally to the defense of anybody threatened with censorship, whether hard-core pornographer or inciter to riot. Not our concepts, but ourselves are threatened. If our aim as writers were to communicate our opinions, we could usually come to terms with society about matters of taste and timing, we could distinguish between form and content. But speaking out, publishing, is our existence. To be muffled as writers is tantamount to being choked, jailed, or locked in an insane asylum and driven crazy. Also, since we often cannot ourselves control what springs forth and demands publication, which sometimes is not at all what we wish to say, we cannot be legally responsible, though of course we are esthetically responsible to say it well.

Our situation is paradoxical. We cannot tolerate censorship; yet when there is censorship, we at least know that our speech has energy—it has hit home. Censored, we have the satisfaction of righteous indignation, we can expect the solidarity of our peers, and we can have a fight. When there is no censorship, we feel uneasy, isolated, out on a limb. For once the act of authorship in which we were engaged and alive is past, we are not sure that we exist. The artwork that we have produced gives no satisfaction to us, for the better it is, the less it was ours.

CHAPTER III

Speaking and Language

So far in these remarks about not speaking and speaking, speaking as action and speech as a thing, I have talked as little as possible about language. But speakers speak language, and speech is heard as the common language. Nevertheless, when I now bring the common language into the discussion, I intend to maintain the same emphasis or bias: that the speakers and hearers are active and shaping. They intervene in the world and are in the world in a special way as speakers. And what they primarily act on and shape is the inherited code that they have learned in their speech-community—in order to say what needs to be said, their meaning. The code is given to speakers and it forms them, including what they can mean. But the power to speak and hear continually modifies the code to say sentences that do mean. And language is not the code but these sentences.

Maintaining this emphasis on speaking, I will go strongly against the grain of most of the linguists of the past fifty years—the cultural anthropologists, positivist grammarians, rationalistic structuralists, and theorists of Communications. They like to dwell on the code as constant, supra-individual, and generalized. But the language of speakers is various and modifying, interpersonal and personal, situational and concrete. And *this* is how they communicate. In my opinion, the abstract recorded code is a fetish of linguists, and sometimes it is an artifact of their methods of investigation and analysis. (I will spell out my dissent in Chapter VI.) Indeed, I would prefer to say: Language is not an *instrument* of communication between speaker and hearer, it is their *communication*—their transaction—as speaker and hearer.

A corollary of the constant code of the linguists is that the forms of language are not altered by the meanings of the speakers, and the forms themselves do not properly "mean" anything. But it can be shown that forms and meanings continually affect one another. In my opinion, these linguists do not understand how *language* has meaning. Meaning is the end-in-view of *speaking and hearing;* it is not something extrinsic to speech. Meaning is not thoughts or purposes in the heads of the speakers, and it is not, as Bloomfield said, the relation of events prior to their speaking and consequent to their speaking. Meaning is what needs to be said in coping with the actual situation of the speaker and hearer, so far as it can be done by saying. Meaning is not *conveyed* by speech or *pointed to* by speech; it is speaker and hearer making sense to one another in a situation.

In good colloquial or literary speech, meaning is explicit in the sentences and can very often be shown by how the speakers have distorted the code, especially when the code is inadequate, as it very often is.—"Correct speech,"

speech according to the code, tends to have less meaning.
—Conversely, we cannot finally understand the forms of
language—whether the pronunciation, the grammar, or the
vocabulary—apart from what wants to be said, the meanings.

1

There are limits, at opposite extremes, of speakers'
uses of the common code: A speaker may be unable to
speak, or the code may be inadequate for what he needs to
say. Let us consider these in turn and then go on to the
realm where there is a better match and speakers use the
code and modify it.

For a natural speaker like man, inability to speak is
usually the result of an injury, or it is psychopathological
or sociopathological in the situation. He may be aphasic or
lisp, stutter, be embarrassed or confused. The language may
be foreign to him. (I will say something about aphasia in
Chapter V.)

Lisping might, for instance, indicate a "pre-dental character," one who because of his mischances in weaning has
never grown up to bite something off, and this same in-
decisiveness (from *caedo,* "cut") will show up in his other
behavior. The man who says "er . . . er . . ." while he
searches for words has what F. S. Perls used to call a hang-
ing-on bite: He won't let mama go, even though no milk
is flowing. We have talked about the man who lapses into
long silences, "thinking," while he chews his molars.

Stuttering is rarely as physiological as this; rather there
is something amiss in relation to the interlocutor. A stut-
terer may not stutter with his peers, but when he is afraid
of being tested, ashamed of being exposed, unable to meet
a teacher's expectation. Susan Goodman says that, in stut-

tering, there is a positive interruption by a split-off part of the personality that wants to get hold of the speech organs to say something different; it is a situational schizophrenia. Then the natural therapy would be to relearn how to be in such situations without internal conflict.[1]

Let us try to be precise about what can be said about language from such pathologies. The form or meaning of words is not given by body actions. Words with t's do not onomatopoetically express biting. The common code *is* supra-individual and conventional. But when speaking breaks down, we can see the animal powers and interpersonal relations that are actualized when we *can* speak. To say the phoneme, you have to be able to bite; and if you can't bite, there may well be a restriction in what you can *mean,* e.g. it is likely to show up in other behavior. Negatively, the defect predicts something definite, though, of course, with a low probability—a psychotherapist would look for a syndrome with many traits. Positively, the animal or interpersonal ability tells us nothing definite, yet it is always, as potentiality, part of the definition of speaking and therefore of language. We do not usually mention such abilities, but they are necessary conditions and essentially relevant. There is a famous question: "What general thinks of the law of gravity as part of the art of strategy?" And the answer is: "The great one."

Most frequently, a pathology is seen when the person speaks poorly. An embarrassed adolescent peppers every sentence with "you know," "I mean," "you know what I mean." People avoid commitment to their own words or avoid confronting the others, by using devices of indirect statement. Instead of saying "Cut it out!" they might say

---

1. The genteel stammer common in the British House of Lords is an interesting variant. It is no doubt partly put on to play the amateur, to hold attention, to take one's time with complete self-assurance: Let them wait.

"You're getting me angry," or "I'm getting angry with you," or "It makes me angry when people etc."—and this last might even be said quietly or with a smile. A man modestly prefaces every remark with "In my opinion," as if he were the Pope and ever spoke but his opinion. Instead of saying what they think or even "I think that . . . ," people say "It strikes me that . . . ," "One has the impression that. . . ." Instead of "Give me" or "I want," they say "Naturally everybody wants" or worst of all, they leave it up to you to guess what in the devil they want. People in quite desperate situations cannot say "Help me!" but they phrase a question, "Could you help me?"—so I am sure that the imperative mood is a direct action and does not have a "you" understood.

The use of "Well——" to introduce a reply when called on belongs to all of us. It is puzzling just what part of speech it is: adjective? adverb? introjection? It seems to make a buffer to the other person's speech while one shifts gears to one's own. A more efficient buffer is to repeat the other's question in one's own voice: "What is my opinion about HR 105? Well——" Then the subsequent answer can proceed as if one is talking to oneself. There is also the aggressive opposite device: (A) "Please pass the salt." (B) "You need the salt!" "You want my opinion on HR 105!" This is used by parental types who express your thoughts for you and take control of the situation.

We can make a scale of levels of withdrawal from engaging in dramatic interaction with the other person:

(o) If the situation allows, the person simply acts and says nothing.

(1) The speaker says what he means, including his feelings. For instance, he makes an angry demand: "Scram!"

(2) More weakly, he puts the feeling itself into words: "I'm getting angry. You'd better scram."

(3) He generalizes, conceptualizes, explains: "It makes me angry when. . . ." "Anybody would get angry when. . . ."

(4) Finally, he uses talk that by-passes both his feelings and what he wants: "You and I seem to have a semantical difference. . . ."

For most linguists, all these are plausible English and even plausibly equivalent in meaning. But they're not.

We can, of course, make a similar scale for avoiding talking about a subject matter. One can write, "Living on a farm, he has a secure and satisfying life," or one can write, as I have, "Living on a farm, he gets security and life-satisfaction." One can write, "He likes to make love" or "He is motivated by sexual desire." Needless to say, this is a painful theme for people like me who write sociology. I am often appalled at the sentences that I have let pass. Pascal said, "There is a time to call Paris Paris and a time to call it the capital of the kingdom." He was right, and it is never the same time, even though according to Bertrand Russell's logic the expressions are equivalent.

2

At the other extreme, the speaker may be all there, but the language is inadequate to say his say. This continually happens when we are being animal or highly emotional, and we compensate by gestures, grimaces, various grunts and clicks, or we slam the door in frustration. Erwin Straus has an exquisite essay on sighing, showing that this puzzling behavior is the effect of a despair that no longer wants to breathe because it does not want energy in a hopeless case, yet one simply must breathe; so one exhales through constricted channels. There is no code word for this common condition. But feelingful natural signs often do occur in language as onomatopoetic introjections; e.g. in his *Expression of the Emotions,* Darwin gives a good physiological etiology for the common "Oh!" of startlement or astonishment.

Coming out to the croquet court with a mallet and a ball, he says, "Oh . . . ah." "Oh" when he notices, surprised, that his opponent has brought two balls; "ah" when he catches on, remembers that each player is to play two balls and he must go back for another.

Ferdinand de Saussure points out that onomatopoetic words are never organic elements of a linguistic system. I doubt that this is absolutely true—I cannot think of a good example of syntax governed by an onomatopoeia: "Ah that he were alive!" the example is factitious, and there might be a better one. But surely Saussure's remark is largely true. Its importance, however, is that it points to a serious defect in language—at least modern language—not because onomatopoeia is important, but because the animal basis of interjections is important and ought to be able to be said structurally. Poets contrive to make interjections an organic part of their language by inverting the word order, distorting the syntax, and adding rhythm and resonance. Ordinary folk in a passion give up on the language.

If we turn to the more fundamental issue, however, of not whether imitative onomatopoeia has a structural effect, but whether physiological natural signs have such an effect, there is no doubt that they do. The forcefulness of imperatives, the voice-fall at the period of declaratives, the rising tone of interrogatives—these are certainly in part natural signs; we can show correlates to them in the breathing, eyes, brows; and they have correlates in the grammar. As natural signs they have more power to communicate than the "correct" grammar: "You are *going!*" is an imperative, though the form is declarative; "you are going?" is a question, though the word order is not. My point is not that grammatical form, e.g. inverting the word order for questions, has any symbolic expressiveness—it might be an arbitrary convention—but that what needs saying will single out some variation to say it, and it can and will continue to find such variations or it will invent them.

One can make a list of "secondary phonemes," as Bloomfield calls them—emphases, rising inflections, and so forth—to domesticate the variations into the common code, but colloquial speakers will then vary also the established variations when they need to. "You are going," said quietly, can be even more imperative than "You are *going!*" Speakers are disposed to use the forms that have become established and are "correct"; but this is not because they are arbitrary, which they are, but because they are expressive enough, so long as they are. At the point where established forms cease to be expressive enough, natural signs will reappear. It is a reasonable inference that they are always there, underlying. It has become the custom of linguists to call "paralinguistic" such items as go beyond the recorded code—gestures, new emphases, and so forth. This is a dodge. They are language.

As we have already mentioned in discussing silence, language fails a speaker when he wants to say what is too complicated, subtile, high, unique, or mysterious. The language of metaphysics, as Wittgenstein says, is "peculiar." The sweet talk of talkative lovers sounds like novels or poems they have read or, alas, movies they have seen. Subtile feelings may have to be said in music. Theology is illogical and often ungrammatical. Mystical experience says nothing. In my plays I sometimes bring angels onto the scene, and if, in their exalted moments, they have to say something, I give them a string of nonsense syllables, which the protagonist answers in kind if he catches their drift. This is a drastic modification of English.

Most often words do not fail a speaker; rather, he wrenches the words a bit and communicates. This does not mean that the constant supra-individual code is unimportant; on the contrary, it is all the more indispensable. Unless the speakers know the code well, they do not hear the modifications. Bloomfield speaks of "the fundamental assumption of linguistics, namely: In certain communities [speech-communities] some speech-utterances are alike as to form and meaning." But it is how the speaker varies the code—by his style, the rhythm and tone of his feeling, his simple or convoluted syntax, his habitual vocabulary—that is *his* meaning, his meaning *in the situation,* which is all the meaning there is. This should be a platitude, except that it tends to be denied or brushed aside by linguists.

3

Turn now to the domain where there is a good match between speaking and code. A man has something to say, the common code is adequate to say it, and using the code he communicates with another. Speaking, he reports what he saw or did, gives directions, asks or answers a question, buys something, commands a service, explains a situation or how something works. Listening, he readily grasps what is said, is told what he needs to know, hears the news, what is for sale, who has called him. It is a vast domain and contains many vital uses of speaking. By it all transactions in the public environment are made possible. Business offices and all kinds of institutions—whatever their essence as magic, violence, love, or greed—run from day to day on easy communication by a common code. As Sapir summarizes it, "The content of every culture is expressible in its language." (Except, I suppose, the animal or mystical conventions of the culture.)

It is with this domain that Roman Jakobson—or the telephone company—is concerned when he says,

> The communications engineer most properly approaches the essence of the speech event when he assumes that the optimal speaker and listener have at their disposal more or less the same "filing cabinet of prefabricated representations"; the addressor selects one of these preconceived possibilities and the addressee is supposed to make an identical choice from the same assembly of possibilities already foreseen and provided for.

In another passage, describing every speaker rather than the "optimal," Jakobson spells out this concept of communication. There is

> an ascending scale of freedom: in phonemes zero; in coinage of words marginal; in the forming of sentences, the speaker is less constrained; in the combination of sentences, freedom rises substantially.

Jakobson would say that this obtains for most situations of speaking.

I don't think so. Rather, only a small fraction of the actual talk that goes on is exchanging this kind of cut-and-dried information or is exchanging information in this way. And there is only a small part of that fraction that does not drastically tamper with the code, in sound, in grammar, and in nuances of meaning. It is not that either the speaker or the code is inadequate, but that for most purposes speaking is a far freer business than Jakobson describes; nor is most communication like exchanging file cards. Language is not code. Communication is not exchanging "information," except in a vastly extended meaning of the term.

To be understood, people say the phonemes within tolerable limits of accuracy, but situations determine what the tolerable limits are. We are used to our friends, and the context makes their sentences clear; in another set-up we have to speak "clearer." We readily vary our pronunciation in style in different milieus, for instance in different class milieus, sometimes with snobbery and condescension, but usually quite insensibly, just to be a right guy. Depending on speed of speech or passion of feeling, we utter different sounds. The coefficient of freedom is well above zero. Ellipsis, redundancy, and "bad" grammar are the rules in actual speech, not the exceptions. Fragmentary phrases and dangling afterthoughts. What needs to be said is often propositional in the situation, e.g. "No, *that* one"; it is not propositional in a verbal subject and predicate. It seems to me to be an unnecessary, and improbable, assumption that such fragments are always elliptical transforms of full sentences; it is more likely that they never had to become full sentences. People know many more words than they use but rule out most of them as inappropriate. Colloquial and transient usages abound, and only they are correct etiquette. Meaning is said not according to the dictionary, often not by words altogether. Yet it must be called language because it flows without a ripple in and out of the rest of the stream of language.

A moment's reflection will show that it must be so. Vital as they are, reports, directions, announcements, definite questions and answers in public places, these constitute a small part of life; but speaking pervades every part of life. And as communication—not to speak of other uses of speech—an unmodified code has fatal defects. For intimate intercourse, "correct" speech does not say enough. Communication depends heavily on speed and timing, style, private meanings, short cuts, laughing, grunts, and gestures. "The more the subject of a dialogue is held in common," said Tolstoy (quoted by L. S. Vygotsky), "the more probable it is that speech will be condensed and abbreviated." No point in maintaining public manners, any more than in dress. But such speech is not like taking your hat and tie off; it is like never having put them on.

Here is a typical snatch of talk I heard yesterday. She: "*You*—swimmin?" I (offended): "Why not?" He: "Brrr. Tscold." The pronunciation was poor; some of the phonemes were impossible in English; the grammar was rudimentary; the communication was excellent.

Spatial factors, for instance, are crucial. They may themselves be conventional and part of the common code; thus it is necessary, as Edward Hall has determined with careful measurements, to maintain the right loudness at the right distance for intimate talk, ordinary conversation, public utterance, public oratory; otherwise people simply cannot listen to what is said.[2] But these ratios, too, are different in different momentary situations, e.g. a loudness that is acceptable and hearable in an angry moment would be unacceptably pompous at other times and soon not heard.

Consider the following examples. She, having just spoken on the phone, says in a quite loud voice, "Mike is coming on Friday"—her sentence is regular in every respect, but it is just this, the tone of the announcement, *including the exceptional correctness of the pronunciation and grammar,* that communicates the important message. Because the sentence is "correct," it means "Mark. I am saying something exceptional." Similarly: "Want a fried egg?" "No, I'll have some breakfast later"—the spelled-out correctness of the reply means that a friendly offer is

2. "3–6 inches, soft whisper, top secret. 8–12 inches, audible whisper, very confidential. 12–20 inches, soft voice, confidential. 20–36 inches, soft voice, low volume, personal subject matter. 4½–5 feet, full voice, non-personal. 5½–8 feet, slightly overloud, public information for others to hear. Across the room, loud, speech to group." (Edward Hall)

being duly appreciated. To be "correct" is to be exceptional.

We pronounce differently at different speeds. But here is a pretty example, culled from Defoe by Otto Jespersen, where the time it takes to say a sentence requires twisting the grammar too: "God made the world, and you, and I, and all things"—given the slow enumeration, "me" would here sound ungrammatical, and it would not really say the message that it is *we,* we persons, who are creatures.

The architectural plan or stage setting in which a discourse occurs is an essential factor in the kind of speech. In religious rituals, there is a difference between the use of speech by a priest acting as the foremost of the congregation and performing the sacrifice facing the Host, and the Protestant preacher of the Gospel facing the congregation because his words are themselves the sacrament; and both of these are different from the sacramental silence of the Quakers facing one another, when the words may or may not come. There is a different syntax, and theory of therapy, in the Freudian psychoanalysis where the patient makes a free-associating monologue to an unseen and silent therapist, and the supportive conversation of a Sullivanian physician and patient facing one another across a desk. Some savage primitives eat in silence, apart from the common cook-fire communing with their biological juices; this is a different silence from the social isolation of busy Americans at a lunch counter; and both are different from the animated but not serious conversation that (in good cases) occurs around a friendly dinner table as the natural effect of satisfying food.[3]

Nor is the abstract code apt for conveying truth of a more universal kind, whether scientific or ethical. It is nothing but past language, and it contains embedded in it

3. I take these examples from an old essay on "Seating Arrangements," in *Utopian Essays.*

the common prejudices, idols of the tribe and marketplace, and bad metaphysics of its culture.[4] Every living group of people, according to its own common sense and its current prejudices, will selectively taboo some words, use others sarcastically, redefine others. Scientists and craftsmen, when they want to be precise, forsake the common code for their trade words, diagrams, and symbols. All people, when they want to speak earnestly on philosophical or religious matters, resort to being incoherent, ungrammatical, and redundant. Talking in the code does nothing to effect people's values, fixed ideas, or neurotic attitudes; when we try to reach a person in psychotherapy or education, or at critical junctures in personal life, we try to get him to alter his use of the common code, and we must speak otherwise ourselves.

There is a common code because in a society all speakers do or may impinge, and we must also communicate with the distant and the dead. But even in this respect, homogeneous speech must not be overstressed. According to recent investigation (C. J. Bailey, 1971), creole situations are not freakish but are "commoner than not."

In any case, the public common environment is not where most of life is lived. The environment of an organism is always *its* environment. Unless they are lonely, most people talk mostly to family, friends, neighbors, fellow workers. And their language is what I have been describing: They use some words of the common store (although they know very many more); they use many of

4. An obvious example is the sexual prejudice embedded in English. Consider two examples from this book: " 'Let the child be,' meaning 'Leave him alone as he is,' " and "One just speaks and makes sense as he goes along." In the first case, I can imagine a feminine writer saying, "Leave her alone as she is"; but it would be extremely odd to write, "One speaks and makes sense as she goes along." The logical expression would be, "One speaks and makes sense as one goes along," but it isn't colloquial English.

these with their own nuances; they somewhat use the correct grammar; their pronunciation is often wildly deviant, but their friends can make it out. They shade, weight, modify, and interpret these linguistic elements according to their shared experience and community concerns. Besides, every good colloquial speaker, like every good writer, develops his own style—the system of modifications that works for him and says his say.

At no point, however, would we call such intimate or stylish speech a dialect or sub-language. The speakers can understand the common code, they speak it when they want to, and they select freely from it. But the converse is not true; the code is not adequate to what needs to be said; it is not the language.

4

It is extraordinary how for nearly fifty years—really, almost everybody after Jespersen—linguists have soft-pedaled these obvious facts. Style used to be treated in Rhetoric, but nobody studies this kind of rhetoric. It is now (amateurishly) treated in General Semantics. But it is essentially Linguistics, for it permeates the sounds, the grammar, and the lexicon, and it is the actuality of most natural language. Instead, with ingenuity and fantastic detail, linguists have devoted themselves to the code, "what the speakers have in common," though indeed it might not frequently occur as natural language—and in some of its constructed forms I doubt that it has ever occurred. I would suggest that the subject matter of Linguistics is something actual and universally common, namely: the relation, often the tension, that exists between a speaker's power to speak and the code of the speech-community; and the relation, often the tension, between a speaker's need to say his say and the need to be clear to the hearer. These relations and tensions produce language.

5

Cultural anthropologists set great store by pattern, and language is part of the determining pattern. They emphasize how it socializes the children, determines the tribal metaphysics, and is part and parcel of the technique. Sapir says that the content of a culture is expressible in its language. Benjamin Whorf takes it a step further: that the ideas of the culture are only such as can be expressed in the language. And for both, the language is fixed. This poses a curious dilemma.

If culture and code go so closely together and if the code determines what can be thought, felt, and valued, then it becomes impenetrable how a person from a different culture can ever understand anything across the boundary, e.g. how can I get anything out of Homer or Sophocles? How does Whorf understand the Hopi? Cf. Sapir:

> Human beings are very much at the mercy of the particular language which has become the medium of expression for their society. No two languages are sufficiently similar to represent the same social reality. The worlds in which different societies live are distinct worlds.

And Whorf:

> We dissect nature along lines laid down by our native language. We ascribe significance as we do largely because we are parties to an agreement to organize it in this way, an agreement that holds throughout our speech community and is codified in the pattern of our language. The agreement is unstated, but its terms are absolutely obligatory.

To my mind, the solution of the dilemma is simple. The common code is not identical with the power to speak and the actual speech of individuals, intimate groups, and functional groups, and the latter is normally always still plastic—it shapes the code as well as being shaped by it. The bother with the anthropologists' formulations is in the terms "medium of expression," "represent reality," "ascribe significance," "pattern of language"; language is not a lifeless tool, but an act of coping. Thus, with reading, teachers, and consulting my own feelings and fantasies, it is not impossible for me to cross the boundary and get something out of Homer. It is because our power of speech is *not* in absolute correspondence with its code that we can pick up another way of saying things and tell it to ourselves, and so begin to understand the other culture—especially when, lo! in the other culture we find human actions that are relevant to ourselves.

Whorf has a quite different solution: it is to be a detached anthropologist who, by understanding linguistic determinism, can discount the opacity of language: "The person most free would be a linguist familiar with many languages." This is the Philosopher Linguist like Plato's Philosopher King or Frank Lloyd Wright's Philosopher Architect. But I doubt that it will give us Homer. Rather, it is by the language of *Homer,* by the *language* of Homer, that we get something out of Homer.

I do agree with another thesis of Whorf's, however, that sprang from his character and life rather than his amateurish speculation: A culture shock must precede getting something out of the other culture. Unless we first experience, with displeasure, resistance, and wonder, how people are different—and the experience changes ourselves—we will not come to see how they are like. Nor will their texts ever make organic sense. The simplest, and obvious, reading of a foreign text often seems very odd at first. The more obvious it gets to be to the professor, the more exasperated he becomes that the students cannot dig it.

If some statements of the cultural anthropologists are taken literally, there is a kind of psychoneurotic who would be quite normal. This is the man who obsessionally translates into the code, who talks like a dictionary and is semantically accurate and phonetically correct, rather than just speaking. Physiologically, he may talk above his held breath and inhibit his chest tones, with a flat effect that he calls "objectivity." He is like the kind of bad driver who, instead of sitting *in* his car and driving it as an extension of his body, manipulates the machine as if from outside; instead of spontaneously stopping at a red light as if it were a real obstacle, he interprets the light as a signal to be decoded "Stop" and then stops. So instead of speaking, our neurotic alienates his speech as a tool that he uses. Then it is hard to know what *he* means to say; indeed, his character is to conceal that, especially from himself. Very little communication takes place. As Norbert Wiener used to say, "The more probable the message, the less information it gives."

Consider the same speech from the listener's point of hearing. Instead of actively listening, catching the speaker's probable drift, guiding himself by it, making his own interpretations, modifications, and short cuts, and appropriating the message as part of his own meaning, he is brought up short by the pedantic monotone. He does not get enough colloquial and non-verbal clues to catch the drift and guide himself. He soon finds that he has to translate the speech into real English in order to listen to it. This is tiresome work, and his attention wanders. The more accurate the statement, the more he fails to hear it. Compare the following, cited by Richard and Roslyn Warren:

William Bryan and Noble Hunter noted that skilled telegraphers did not transcribe the signals that constituted a word until 6 to 12 words after the signals were heard. If subsequent portions of the message could not provide helpful context, as in the case of stock quotations, telegraphers changed their strategy and followed the message more closely in time. Telegraph companies charged higher rates for such messages because they lacked redundant context, were much more difficult to receive, and had to be transmitted more slowly.

Thus, paradoxically, a certain amount of uncertainty and "inefficiency" is necessary for efficient exchange of information, for listening too is active and shaping. Beyond a certain amount of uncertainty, however, the listener cannot catch the drift either.

"By the time a child is six," says Whorf, "the phoneme pattern has become ingrained and automatic. . . . No sequence of sounds that deviates can even be articulated without difficulty." I am at a loss what to make of this assertion. It is without any difficulty whatever that people in various walks of life say, "Schlitz," "shmoo," "schwa," "Gestalt," "shmeer," and "shtunk," though these are not possible English patterns. We say "Brrr" when we are cold, we give Bronx cheers, and we click "ts ts." If you ask somebody to imitate Chinese, he will produce a variety of squeals, unless he is the type of neurotic who cannot produce nonsense syllables at all, since he always has to make sense by cleaving to the code. As in other things, when we *deliberately* try to hit a subtlety that is new to us, we find it very hard. It is hard to pick up the phonemes and lilt of a foreign language by trying. But people apt at foreign languages seem to mimic spontaneously and without self-consciousness, as children learn their native tongues.

If I may make a wicked analogy, the language described by Sapir and Whorf seems like the peculiar dialect of New

York school principals carefully learned, for the Board of Examiners, to provide a standard for the children of immigrants from all Europe in 1890, but that nobody ever spoke on land or sea.

Throughout this period of scientific linguistics, finally, language is defined as not only the instrument of communication, but also as the "means by which men express themselves" (M. W. Bloomfield and L. Newmark, who are structuralists, 1964; Sapir said the same in 1921). It is never clear to me what is intended by "self-expression"; nothing much is said about it except that it is terribly prevalent. It might mean that the speaker wants to say his say without much regard for the listener's response— though I suppose every speaker wants to be understood, to be clear—and that the content of his say is not informative, imperative, or instrumental, but more emotional. Or autobiographical and confessional? In any case, letting off steam and self-revelation are indeed important uses of speaking. The speaker takes part in the institution of public language and has a possible public forum, in order to get something off his chest, confess guilt, alleviate loneliness, alleviate the sense of being abandoned or peculiar. But then I think my previous remarks are even more germane. Especially for self-expression the common code has to be strongly modified, and tends to be. Pain or mourning cannot use the common grammar or word order any more than they can use a neutral tone of voice. Introspection finds the common words imprecise to just one's own case. Eccentricity may not even have the common words.

6

Former anthropologists said much what I have been trying to say. Tyler and Boas used to emphasize how pragmatic and inventive mankind is, and they liked to show

how languages are always made adequate to say what people need to talk about in the conditions of life. If a people can count to only three, they will count to fifteen as soon as there is something worth counting. Rather than language being constant and generalized, Malinowski pointed to linguistic variation in every local and even immediate small group situation.

Older philosophers of language, like Michel Bréal or Jespersen, refused to distinguish so sharply between speaking and language, *parole* and *langue*. They readily saw language being created, molded by its meanings in use. They were intensely interested in the origin of language, a topic which is now universally considered to be ridiculous, all about bow-wow, pooh-pooh, and love calls of birds. Historians of language, e.g. A. C. Baugh, have shown how in some historical situations entrenched grammatical forms easily lapse and in other situations thousands of new words may be added in a generation, sometimes dozens by one writer, two or three on a single page.

Psychiatrists of aphasia, like Hughlings Jackson or Kurt Goldstein, show that language must allow free play. If the pattern is too rigid, people cannot speak at all.

I am entirely with Malinowski, Jespersen, and Goldstein.

Saussure made a distinction between the historical evolution of a language, which shows continual change, and the present cross-section of a language at any time that the speaker speaks, which is fairly constant. This is reasonable, because a speaker speaks the language that he has. But the distinction is misleading if we do not add to it that the speaker is now *speaking* the language and thereby making molecular changes. This is how he *has* his language.[5] The nature of a living language like English cannot be

5. It would be attractive to suggest that Lyell's principle in geology is applicable to linguistics: The forces that are observable in

found by describing, or constructing, the language in the abstract, constant, supra-individualistic, and generalized. It shows itself in the modifications of the code in speaking, in various uses of speech by various kinds of users, in how the language copes with every new situation in its characteristic way.

In the past decade or so, the best linguists have again begun to appreciate the active power of speakers and hearers to form language. The "rationalists," learning from Chomsky, show that speakers derive sentences that are possible only if they have prior principles of grammar —indeed, Chomsky sometimes speaks as if people had a special language faculty, a kind of innate algebra. This is a step in the right direction, but in my opinion it is a misplaced concreteness. The intellectual power of a speaker operates primarily not on strings of sentences but *in* his global experience, in the situation in which he is cast, that includes the inherited code, the hearer, and the need to say his say. The Gestalt that he then forms is language.

(The rationalism of the new structuralists is about at the stage of Descartes or, more accurately, Hobbes. But we must always go all the way to Kant and the "synthetic unity of apperception." Descartes thought there were abstract reasons, in God's mind, e.g. "a circle is the locus of points equidistant from a fixed point." Hobbes thought that we had the reason by constructing it, e.g. rotating a line with one end fixed and describing a circle with the other end. Kant held that we can have experience al-

---

present speaking did form languages and are embedded there, and on-going speaking makes an *evolutionary* difference to the language it speaks. But the subject matters are so disparate that the analogy might be inaccurate. It would have to be shown that the alterations made by a present speaker are additive. Maybe they are—if the impulse to them is general. But I do not have the scholarship to judge by.

together, including space and time, only by actively struc-
turing the given situation; reason is *a priori,* but it is *not*
abstract. Chomsky's transformations sound very much like
Hobbes, but the speech of actual speakers is more like
Kant.)

Older philologists used to look for model examples in
powerful writers, and lexicographers have always done so.
This was not merely snobbery nor due to their training
in Greek and Latin classics; it was a good instinct for the
life of language. Powerful writers are not normative—
indeed, they are often "incorrect"—but they add to meaning, they are authors (from *augere,* "to augment"). They
keep the language alive, just as the drive to slang, "bad
English," keeps the language alive. Inventive speakers,
colloquial or literary, make the language say what it has
not adequately said. What kills language is dull, stereotyped, lazy, or correct speech. There is a tendency of mass
speech to degenerate.

This brings me to a question. Why am I so polemical
about recent language theory, as in this chapter? Why
don't I let those scholars do their thing, while I, as a man
of letters, do mine? Frankly, I am made politically uneasy
by it, by the thrust of cultural anthropology, Basic languages, scientific linguistics, communications engineering,
and the Theory of Communications. They usually treat
human communication as far more mechanical than it is;
they are technological in an antihumanistic sense. They
suit State and corporate policy too well and have crashingly
pre-empted too many research grants and university appointments. My own bias, to be equally frank, is to play
up the animal, spontaneous, artistic, and populist forces
in speech. These forces are both agitational and deeply
conservative—as I think good politics is. And as a writer,
I want to defend literature and poetry as the indispensable
renovators of desiccated and corrupt language.

CHAPTER IV

Sub-Languages

Innumerable sentences that are said are mainly social-cement, keeping people together by engaging in the sociable action of speaking and listening, playing with the common code like any other game, and telling enough information to avoid the pain of a blank mind. Or we can put this in a way that is not quite the same: We are communal animals, an important part of our communal nature is speaking, so when we can we speak. To call it cement describes better the talk in a bar, where people might otherwise be lonely. To avoid blankness of mind is the reason for most reading of newspapers, which must be the largest proportion of all reading. But to call it the chatter of a communal species better describes the small talk of chance meetings on the street or across the back fence, drop-in visits, talk around card tables, ordinary (pleasant) family life, ceremonial dinners.

I have no statistics, but my impression is that, on the whole, small talk sticks closer to the constant and supra-individual code than more concerned or intimate talk. It has more standard subject-predicate sentences and probably better pronunciation, if only because to deviate far from the expected would jeopardize harmony and be bad manners. But by the same token, it is necessary to avoid saying much, whether giving information, explaining, debating, or having any instrumental purpose. Consider a pep talk before a ball game or a political rally during a campaign: The purpose is solidarity for action, to win, to get out the vote. It would be disastrous if anybody made sense.[1]

Harold Garfinkel ran a poignant experiment to show the need actively to *prevent* communication in small talk. He had his students go home and insist on the literal meaning, and truth or falsity, of the chatter. Let me give two excerpts:

> Hi, Ray, how is your girl friend feeling?—What do you mean how is she feeling, do you mean physical or mental?—I mean how is she feeling. What's the matter with *you?*—Nothing. Just explain a little clearer what you want to know.—Skip it. Hey, are you sick?

> All these old movies have the same kind of old iron bedstead in them.—What do you mean? Do you mean all old movies, or some of them, or just the ones you have seen?—What's the matter with you? You know what I mean.—I wish you would be more specific.— Drop dead.

---

1. Previously I gave examples to show that speaking correctly called special attention to the meaning. Here I point out that speaking correctly is useful for not meaning anything. It would seem that speaking correctly has every use except simply communicating! But I don't really believe this. It is an artifact of writing about language; only the interesting sentences get recorded.

1

It is different, however, when this kind of talk is *used* to glue together not people in general, but a specific group, clique, adolescent gang, or thieves' gang. We at once come to a different kind of language, that defines and affirms the group's identity and commits the members to it. There is a willful withdrawal from the common code, creating what amounts to a proper sub-language as a badge. Let me give an extreme example: Adolescents at the University of Hawaii, which is an uneasy place for many of them, speak perfectly good English while they are on campus, even when they are at the same table in the cafeteria; but off campus they will talk only pidgin, and they have scorn for anybody who treasonably speaks English.

A badge language may or may not communicate more accurately or relevantly. Usually such willed languages are pretty weak. A clique attitude depoverishes experience rather than enriching it by making it deep and intimate. In a circle of junkies the sub-language seems (to me at least) to be as appallingly limited as their purposes. Thus, there is an essential difference between such an argot and the selective and intimate use of the common code by family, friends, neighbors, and co-workers. Intimate language develops naturally, to be able to say people's real interests better than the common code can; it does not aim to modify the common code, it just does it. An argot affirms itself, consciously or unconsciously, against the common code. Sometimes, for purposes of self-defense, it tries to be commonly incomprehensible, like thieves' language or jive.

Jespersen made the remarkable empirical observation that a child of immigrant parents may learn the new language at home, but he takes on the accent of his (slightly

older) peer group on the street—that is, as he psychologically draws away from his parents at age five to six, he
models himself on his ideal gang, like putting on a hockey
shirt and speech is the badge. Speaking is here again a
direct act, naming, self-naming, self-appointing. (Wittgenstein points out that naming is not yet part of the "language game" for a logician.) The same can be seen with
adults who are sexually infatuated or infatuated with a
political cause and unconsciously mimic a new accent and
speech rhythm; but these adult cases are more pathetic,
for such a commitment is not likely to last long—if speech
is labile, so is character.

Contrariwise, the children of immigrants may, as they
grow older, retain or revert to some of the old language—
perhaps their parents' foreign accent—as a self-naming defensive maneuver against assimilation. It is a return of the
repressed. They may rationalize that the old language has
phrases that say what the common language can't say, and
which, of course, affirm their feeling of having a special
cast of mind. Jews have done a lot of this. Urban blacks
claim that their Southern language and country food have
soul. The Jews are a striking case in that, as a people in
exile, their own common code was already a self-naming
amalgam—Yiddish or Ladino—and the revived Israeli
Hebrew must itself for a time be a self-conscious language,
though no longer a sub-language.

It is the factor of artificial boundaries, whether willed
or resignedly recognized, that makes a sub-language. A
Yiddish or Black English spoken spontaneously, as by a
child, is a creole or mixture, but it is a native tongue like
any other. But will, pride, suspicion, and fear are a bad
way to be in the world linguistically as otherwise.

2

When the rich become squeamish and the poor become a caste, social classes develop sub-languages. So long as decent poverty is possible, poor people may have an exceptionally good intimate language selected from the common code—concrete, realistic, and feelingful—at least as good as any other speech in the society. Wordsworth famously singled out the language of "humble and rustic life" as the source for his poetic diction, because it came from a beautiful scene and natural affections, it was under less restraint and was plainer, it was "far more philosophical . . . because such men hourly communicate with the best objects from which the best part of language is originally derived"; whereas the upper and middle classes and the new industrial proletariat were bitched up in various ways. During the same era Jefferson wanted to rely politically on freeholding yeomen for their independence, morality, and democracy. And a little later, Marx singled out the Elizabethan yeomanry as the best condition so far achieved by humanity.

City poverty, too, has had good language, slangy, polyglot, rapid, and argumentative. The common people of Rome, Paris, and New York have all been written up as vivid talkers. They interrupt you in the middle of a sentence because they know all about it beforehand, and often they do. But here too, in order to choose what suits them out of the common code, people have to be free in their own homes and neighborhoods and have to have access to the rest of society.

The case is very different in depressed rural areas or big city slums, where the poor are powerless, segregated, unable to get into the inflationary general economy, unskilled to cope with a centralized high technology, and many of the city youth are the children of uprooted rural migrants. The common code may then be pretty useless to them as a basis for practical communication. Consider a sad example: Large numbers of Spanish-speaking kids in the New York public schools apparently speak English quite fluently to talk about public nonsense, but they cannot say, "I am hungry," "I have a toothache," "My pal is dying in the basement." They have to say these in Spanish, but then the teacher or cop does not know what they are talking about. In the recent trial of Black Panthers in New Haven, the defense attacked the disproportion of whites on the jury rolls because, as their linguistic experts put it, "blacks had developed a significant and unique nonverbal form of communication" and "whites were apt to miss or misunderstand meanings of the Black English dialect and the voice inflections unique to black communication."

As a native speaker of his own dialect, a poor black child has, of course, as much linguistic power as any other child; he has plenty of Chomsky's innate algebra. To borrow examples from Labov: If he says, "He a'way' look' fo' trouble when he red [past tense of "read"] de news," he obviously uses "look' " as past; and although he says, "It John book," he can say, when necessary, "It *is* John's." In the history of English, indeed, there has been a secular tendency to drop the case endings and soft-pedal the copula, so that this dialect is not even out of the mainstream.

But under conditions of alienation, there develops a self-defensive and self-affirming sub-language *against* the common code, a language to fit the sub-"culture of poverty," as Oscar Lewis used to call it, which is not an independent culture. Consider when the children go to an official school. They do not really use the dominant code. They are not allowed to use their own dialect, and certainly they are not encouraged to improve it. Then they are made to feel stupid, as if they did not have intellectual powers.[2] Humanly, they have no alternative but to affirm their language all the more tenaciously. But then they have still less access to the common goods. The situation is explosive.

3

Dialects and creoles are simply languages. Intimate language is superior language; it gives everybody more articulate experience and so enriches the common code too. But class sub-languages thin out every class's experience and language and depoverish the common code.

Basil Bernstein has a profound but confused study of the differences of syntax between lower class and middle class children in London. Let me quote some of his comparisons:

> [Poor children use] short sentences, poor syntax, active voice, repetitive use of conjunctions, no subordination, limited use of adjectives and adverbs, infrequent use of "one" or "it" as subjects, stereotyped idioms. [Middle class children use] accurate order and syntax, complex construction, frequent use of prepositions for logical, temporal, and spatial relation, frequent use of "I," discriminating use of adjectives and adverbs.

2. "Correcting" a child's language, as if he did not have a proper language, is identical with the theory of Head Start that disadvantaged children need special training for their intellectual faculties to prepare them for learning. "But there is nothing wrong with their intellectual faculties; they have learned to speak and can make practical syllogisms very nicely if they need to and are not thwarted. If black children do not have the patterns to succeed in school, the plausible move is to change the school rather than to badger the children" (*New Reformation*, p. 83).

These terms, so far, are rather value-laden; yet I think there is truth in them: What they imply is that speech is not so big a deal for the communication of London poor children as for London middle class children. In fact, poor children—not only in London—do an enormous amount of punching, nudging, hand-stroking in lieu of speaking, whereas this almost never occurs in the middle class. And the lower class child will use many more phrases to ask for his speech to be validated, like "you see?" "you know what I mean?" whereas the middle class child takes speech more for granted as asserting what it says.[3]

Bernstein gives a typical comparative sequence of sentences. The lower class mother says, "Sit down.—Why?—Because I say so." The middle class mother says, "Sit down.—Why?—Because you're a big boy, you see how all the other people are doing." And he explains, "By expressing direct authority, the lower class language tends to discourage the experience of guilt; in middle class language the child's intent becomes important." Also, "the lower class child is not given much instrumental teaching"—at least in words, although he may be shown as much—"whereas the middle class child is continually verbally exposed to connection and sequence, and if one set of reasons is challenged, another set of reasons is elicited." In general,

> Lower working class children have a society limited to a form of spoken language in which complex verbal procedures are made irrelevant by the system of non-verbal closely-shared identifications—plus more naked, less internalized authority. . . . Inherent in the middle class linguistic relationship is a pressure to verbalize

3. I do not think that the child's "you know" is the same as the "you know" of embarrassed adolescents. The adolescents are doubtful that they have a world to assert; the child has a world, but he is not sure that speaking is the way of asserting it.

feeling in an individual manner. To make explicit subjective intent . . . The lower class child learns a form of language which symbolizes the norms of a local group, rather than the individuated experience of its members.

All this is beautifully analyzed. It is not hard to fill in the economic background of both groups, and he tells us something very important about the psychology of verbalizing. But then, unfortunately, Bernstein concludes that the middle class speech is far superior. I don't think so. *Both* are defensive languages. Each has its virtues, which are not class virtues but human virtues: The poor child's speech has the human virtues of animality, plainness, community, emotional vulnerability, and semantic bluntness (though not frankness—they are frightful little liars); the middle class child's speech has the human virtues of prudence, self-reliance, subtile distinction, the ability to move abroad, and responsibility to the verbal truth (but they are already terrible little hypocrites). In both types, however, we can see developing the outlines of pathological speech. The poor kid has to prove his potency; if his stereotyped sentence is not accepted at face value, he has no back-up, is acutely embarrassed, and bursts into tears; he has to diminish anxiety by impulsive reactions and can become totally confused and lose all prudence; he becomes stupid out of spite. The other kid escapes from physical and emotional contact by verbalizing; he speaks correctly to control his spontaneity; he rationalizes and deceives himself; his consciousness of "I" isolates him and makes him needlessly competitive; he is guilt-ridden.

The poor kid's use of language does not get him enough of the cushioning protection that symbolic action can give; as Kurt Goldstein puts it, he is liable to catastrophic reactions. But the other lives too much by language; he tries to make it do more than it can or should, and so he immobilizes himself and loses vitality. (We shall return to these two types in the next chapter.)

Bernstein says, "Middle class children will have access to both forms of speech, which will be used according to the social context." Yet C. J. Bailey categorically says just the opposite: "It is known that speakers of a prestige idiom have genuine problems in understanding a fairly similar idiom of low prestige, that do not exist on the other side." It is possible that both authors may be superficially correct, but from my limited experience, in street and campus troubles, I think they are both profoundly wrong. Neither group has much access. It is plausible that the lower speakers may hear the upper speakers better because the latter's speech is more articulate and more like the standard speech of, for instance, the mass media. It is plausible that the upper group would find the lower speech simpler and something like their own careless speech.[4] But though the lower speakers hear the others' words, they do not really hear the distinctions, the concessions, the subordinations, and the abstractions; they quickly dismiss it as all bullshit. And the upper speakers are fatally put off by the bluntness and violence, much of which is ritual insult precisely to calm things down; they take the stereotypes too literally; they think that because the language is childish, the reasoning is—but it's not. When the atmosphere heats up, communication breaks down badly.

The goal of education must be for children to regain their free speech without class limitations. (I don't know whether class conflict should be moderated or not, but it should make sense.) There are two possible strategies. The teacher can go along with the child's sub-language as he has it and help him to say and do more with it. This has

4. In this particular comparison, also, Cockney is possibly unusually more inarticulate, compared to Bailey's American "lower class speech."

been the line of a number of teachers in American ghetto schools and of Paolo Freire in Brazil, whether to help poor kids write poetry or to formulate political demands. Or the teacher can try, like Sylvia Ashton-Warner teaching reading to little Maoris, to evoke from the children their own primary words, rising from their fear, hunger, loneliness, and sexuality—in effect, to live through the old traumas in the more favorable circumstances of her school. But note that such efforts are made with lower class children. I have not heard of anything comparable to liberate the speech of middle class children, and if the attempt were made it would be strongly resisted by middle class parents and school authorities.

4

The mighty development of our language from Old English may be instructively regarded as winning its way from being colonized as a sub-language. Twice it was touch and go—during the Danish conquest and especially the Norman conquest. In Walter Scott's classical illustration, the French conqueror said, "beef," "veal," "pork," "mutton," "meat," for the food on the table; the English, who did the farm work, said, "ox," "calf," "swine," "sheep," and "flesh," and these might have become debased words. But luckily the language was creolized instead. Class boundaries were broken and the language was enriched. (In effect, it happened a third time, with the influx of academic Latin during the Renaissance.) "The introduction of French words into English," Baugh points out, "followed the adoption of English by the upper classes"— when the élite gives up its squeamishness, it can do some good as well as harm.

One may meditate also on the *absence* of mixing where

it might have been expected, the paucity of Celtic in Old English or of Red Indian words in American English—but they are not so rare as references to Red Indian people in classical American literature.

5

Much of slang is first invented as a neologism of a gang or special group, e.g. "take the rap" or "kibitzer," yet it comes into circulation as slang precisely by breaking out of its sub-culture. When the boundary is broken, there is a different kind of language, not self-naming and defensive but common and wild. For instance, if a group becomes generally interesting or newsworthy, some terms of its language may become widespread, because they are topical; and they may prove to be colorful, exciting, or to have a valuable new nuance of meaning. Usually they are transient; sometimes they become a permanent part of the common code. As we saw, a Jewish second generation kept many Yiddish words as part of its identity; but since these Jews have been important in entertainment and business, the words have become common slang. Black argot began to become slang through the jazz musicians, but now it has come in strongly through the civil rights and black liberation movements, and the association with blacks by the youth of the white majority.

Slang is not a sub-language. Both sub-language and slang are a violation of the common code. Like Dada in art, they mean to destroy the convention, either for spite or as an act of liberation. (Spite is the vitality of the powerless.) But whereas the sub-language is purposeful—to affirm and defend and be a new code—slang tends to be wildly gratuitous, and it sometimes enriches the common code. For a moment, when slang is introduced, it obliterates altogether the distinction between *langue* and *parole,* given code and spontaneous speaking. So Eric Partridge says, "Slang is the only speech in which linguistic process can be observed in unrestrained activity."

Slang creates new language, just like poetry, and it can be regarded as a kind of folk poetry. "It results," says A. C. Baugh, "from an instinctive desire for freshness and novelty of expression." But in one important respect it is not poetry at all, and this tells us something important about poetry. The speaker of slang still retains the feeling of being "wrong," of breaking the law, of being an individual; but the poet, like every fine artist, is himself the lawgiver—he speaks universally, though he has no warrant whatever. (In Rorschach tests it is hard to distinguish artists from psychopathic personalities.)

Various students of slang all bring out the lawlessness and the language-creating. Whitman says, "Slang is the lawless germinal element below all words and sentences and behind all poetry." Ernest Weekley says, "Phonetic laws have no control over argotic formulations." Carnoy: "Slang is a particular vocabulary in which purposeful fantasy plays a predominant role." Séchrist: "Slang pays no mind to the routine activities of life. It is radical, puts off restraint, but stays close to the objective common-sense world of things." And Partridge mentions acutely, "The instinctive desire to speak bad English."

In these descriptions we are hovering around age two. A child is learning to speak. He tries out his own expressions till he finds the ones that work. He is resentful when he is corrected. He gets the corresponding satisfaction of defying the corrector.

CHAPTER V

Speaking as a Unique Kind of Experience

We have collected enough uses of speaking to see that speaking a language is a very peculiar way of being in the world. Speech is trivial and unimportant except as an instrument of other behavior. Often it is not even an instrument, but mere chatter springing from animal urges. It determines what people can think and how they can behave. It establishes the community of the speakers. It founds institutions and creates binding legal obligations. It is the substance of objects that have independent existence. It is an energy that has physical effects. It is an area of freedom from the compulsion of perception and stimulation.

I have not been able to find any simple concept that defines these divergent and apparently contradictory functions; and I doubt that there is one. Yet it is philosophically unacceptable (to me) to say that some of these uses are essential, *are* speech, and some are inessential or abuses. All are important uses. And in any of them we can usually show that the others are present, as concomitant, or as traces, or as latent and potential.

The case seems to be as follows: Much of our experience is silent perception, both of body and environment, and much is wordless action in the environment. Speech can latch onto almost all experience, including what is silently perceived and wordlessly acted, creating a vast domain of verbalized experience. Much of speaking is also carried on for its own sake, with little connection with other experience. And it is never certain, in a concrete situation and in the act of speaking, how much is using words as part of other experience and how much is just the experience of using words, where the verbalized experience leaves off and just verbalizing begins. So we live in a kind of doubled world, a world of experiences with words attached and a world *made of* experienced words.

Of course, for two millennia, by exploring the meaning of meaning, authors have tried to tie down words to the things they refer to and to establish rules so that the word is not the thing; but I shall show below that in the concrete act of speaking a language there are no such rules—they do not work. Other authors have tried to achieve a prophylaxis of speech by making speech itself a self-enclosed system with its own purely linguistic and logical rules; but I shall show that these rules also do not work—we do not, and cannot, speak without meaning, without referring to other experience. I suggest that it is better to accept the ambiguous situation of the double world as it is and to try to navigate critically within it.

Such a situation, of living in a double world, is rife with delusion. We produce our words with considerable spontaneity and freedom, so we have a kind of control, often a too easy control, of the world with its attached words. Consider the exaggerated statement of Georges Gusdorf, "Man interposes a network of words between the world and himself and thereby becomes the master of the world." But we are not the masters; if we proceed in this way, we sooner or later—and better sooner—get our come-uppance. Nevertheless, the characteristics of speaking and language and speaking a language create a psychological compulsion to the delusion that the word-world has a reality that it does not have. As I spelled out in *Gestalt Therapy* (II,vi), the great evolutionary advances of mankind, like erect posture, speech, and the ability to use tools, have also constituted an accumulating liability to neurosis.

When a speaker speaks about an experience, there is at once an ambiguity as to what of the meaning of his words comes from the experience and what meaning has been added by his speaking. I think this ambiguity is unavoidable. For speaking to achieve what it does, it must risk what it does. Radical language reform to avoid the ambiguity by finding the meaning entirely outside the words, by having the words "point to" the meaning or something like that, is a mistake (see Chapter VII); it makes speaking more mechanical than it can be or ought to be. The only safeguard is old-fashioned humanistic criticism, literary criticism, of the speeches themselves. It has been a mistake to distinguish linguistics sharply from the study of literature. The old philology was wiser.

1

Let us review some of the factors that make speech inevitably seem meaningful, even if it is just words:

(1) All speaking is initiated by the speaker and is at least partly an autonomous act. This is dramatically said in the first mention of human speech in the Bible: God brought the animals to Adam "to see what he would call them"—that is, even God did not know what Adam would say.

Often, speaking has direct physical, institutional, and fictional products, as scientific formulas, legal actions, and poetry. And since social nature imitates art, it is often hard to tell what is real and what is fictional.

Since speaking is spontaneous and latches on to all kinds of experience and structures it to our own speech forms, speech occupies the field first: The burden of proof is always on the nature of things to show that our speaking is irrelevant nonsense, rather than on ourselves to prove that it is not.

(2) Speaking speaks a language, an historical legacy of generations that were busy making sense. So just because we can form a linguistically acceptable sentence, we feel that our action makes sense. Using the code limits our freedom, for our meanings are partly predetermined by the code; but we continually modify the code and re-create history like everything else.

But there is an additional sense of power that comes from the mechanics of speaking a language. Using a code is the motion of an immense nervous machinery, distinguishing the sounds, the grammatical parts, the application of signs to designates: In doing these, our brains are operating as computers more high-powered than any we will manufacture in the foreseeable future. To be sure, none of this immense program would be learned or would survive if it did not somewhat work, reinforced by events and other persons; but during the time our circuits are in operation, we cannot but feel we are doing something meaningful, since we are doing so much.

All perception involves a comparable amount of nerv-

ous activity—and indeed we believe that what we perceive is real—but besides, speech is voluntary; it does not
depend so much on stimuli. Other motor acts, e.g. catching
a ball, require comparable nervous activity and are voluntary, but they are immediately disciplined by material
facts, whereas speech can whirr on and seem to be effective,
whether it is or not.

(3) Grammar of speech always has a close similarity
to what we take to be the nature of things, to the way
we organize experience and have to organize it. Natural
grammars are not, of course, empirically accurate or consistent (*Fräulein* is neuter because *-lein* is, but *nauta* is
masculine though the declension is feminine), but grammar
is never far from epistemology and logic. No matter what
the metaphysical nuances of the concepts in each culture,
the structure of all developed civilized languages, at least,
expresses—in one way or another—quantity, quality, relation, modality, substance, cause, time, space, degree, etc.
—all the categories and conceptual machinery of Kant's
Critique of Pure Reason. Conversely, (Western) "philosophical grammars," that want to be applicable to scientific knowledge, whether ancient, medieval, or modern—
e.g. Aristotle, Thomas of Erfurt, or Carnap—all have a
family resemblance to common syntax and to one another.[1]
If we talk, we talk a rough logic, and if we talk logic we
think we are talking physics.

To avoid using the forms of speech as categories of
experience, recent philosophers have developed both language and logic as formal games with made-up rules. But

1. Thus, in *The Logical Syntax of Language,* Carnap provides
for the universal words "thing," "property," "relation," "condition,"
"process," "action," "spatial point," "temporal point," "temporal
relation," "number," etc. "Necessity," "possibility," "existence," come
in as analytic, valid, or as operators. In brief, it is again very much
Kant's list.

people do not play at speaking or science; they make assertions. I think there is an unavoidable subjective necessity to project grammar into the world.

(4) A speaker has a listener for whom he molds his remarks,[2] and the fact that it is acceptably heard validates his speech. Social pressure can make us distrust even the evidence of our senses—cf. the Asch experiment. Conversely, when our speech is accepted, we take it for meaningful and for real.

Usually we do not have to deny the evidence of our senses to feel that we control reality by our words. We just affirm what we perceive, add on our fantasies, and get legitimation for both by saying them in the common code to ready ears. There is a contract between speakers and hearers that what is said affirms something about reality; it may be a lie or it may be a fiction, but it may not be mere sounds or nonsense.

Thus, it is a principle in progressive psychiatry that the garbled and freakish statements of a psychotic are literal reports out of the real situation he is in, if only we could decipher them. For a time it was the disposition of positivist philosophers to say that many sentences of folk wisdom, metaphysics, and religion were nonsense or at best exclamations; but this went against the grain of common feeling, and the later generation of analytic philosophy has gone back to trying to figure out what people can possibly intend by such remarks.

(5) The more self-conscious speaking is, the more it is like daydreaming, for it is temporarily isolated from the stream of practical behavior. Most speaking, for social-

2. Genesis is again instructive. ii,20 is logically baffling: Adam gave names to the beasts, "but [Hebrew "and"] for Adam there was not found a helpmeet." In the context of the scene it seems to mean that, as the animals parade by two-by-two, only Adam is without a mate. But the more direct meaning seems to be, if you once start talking, you ought to have somebody to talk to.

cement or self-expression, does not involve much conscious-ness; it is enough to have a simple awareness that one is in the world with hearers. But in exchanging information, trying to persuade, introspective self-reporting, or making literature, there is heightened consciousness and deliberate-ness. As William James said, there is heightened conscious-ness when there is interruption in the arc between stimulus and response, when there is a problem, outer or inner. To find the solution, the conscious activity whirrs on by itself.

Freud then pointed out that if interruption and delay become actual frustration, consciousness is heightened to the super-consciousness of daydream and dream, cut off from both body and environment, trying to exhaust in mental activity the energy that cannot otherwise be dis-charged in practical activity. Typically, sexual frustration leads to bright images and masturbation; after an orgasm the images immediately fade. People often similarly ex-haust energy by talking about a situation as if they were coping with it, or they talk as a way of coping with a frustrating situation.

Paradoxically, the very act of making speech more cor-rect and controlled often makes it more delusory.

(6) The "person" who speaks is largely made of words —*persona* is an actor's mask equipped with a megaphone— so he must find that his experience is largely verbalized, for he puts words into what he experiences and therefore finds them there. Personality consists (largely) of one's speech habits—learned because they have worked in spon-taneous acts of speech on many occasions—plus the intro-jection of the common code, mother's and father's voices, voices of childhood peers, and social institutions.

Various psychological explanations come to this same result. For instance, in classical psychoanalysis the ego be-gins to be formed at the time of learning to speak; and the pre-conscious, which is at the disposal of the ego but sealed off from the unconscious, is a repository of words, a lexicon of acceptable wishes and memories that may be recalled by verbal stimuli. In Skinnerian behaviorism, learning to speak occurs by operant conditioning: The infant continually vocalizes with small differences, and the differences are reinforced or obliterated by his parents and other important persons till his speaking is shaped to the common language with his individual variations.

(7) Finally, let me repeat a point made in Chapter II. In order to survive, an animal like man that moves in a continually novel and dangerous environment must have faith that his spontaneous and self-initiating actions are effective in the environment. Speaking is preeminently one of these. A speaker *starts out* with a belief in the magical power of his words.

Combine these factors—the spontaneity of speaking and the need for faith in it, the rules and machinery involved in speaking a language, validation by the community, the propensity to exhaust nervous energy in speech, the largely verbal nature of personality—and we see how people come to exist in a world of signs. The question is how to reduce the error in this human condition, so that sentences can be more true and practical.

It cannot be done by prophylactic rules restricting what use of language is meaningful and what sentence forms are permissible. Such rules, if they were abided by, would make language sterile and unfunctional. (See Chapter VII.) The functional use of words requires that people believe in their meanings, and this belief is in the speaker and hearer—it is not in the relation of the signs and the designates. I doubt that many people mistake the word for the thing; they believe in the words. As Kurt Goldstein says it, "As soon as a man uses language to establish a living relation with himself and his fellows, language is no longer an instrument, a means, but a manifestation, a revelation of his inner being and his psychic ties with the world and his fellows." The cultural anthropologists do not say enough when they say that language is an instrument of communication about the world; speaking language is how the speakers are *in* the world, and it *is* their communication.

But if we accept this human condition, we can then subject actual speeches to criticism, taking account of the likely fallacies. A good maxim is to try out and practice not speaking, in order to have a non-verbalized world to check against the verbal world; this has been a great power of experimental science.

My examples have been taken from the European tradition, but I cannot conceive of any culture speaking any language that will not generate a verbalized world. It is not necessary, however, that this occur with the pathological excess of our own highly verbal culture.

2

Another way of getting at this peculiar normal human condition is to ask what it is like not to have it. Let us again consider two extreme pathological groups: people who cannot speak nor use speech to cope with experience, and people so trapped in speaking that they live mainly verbal lives.

Biologically, to have a domain of speakable experience is a means of homeostasis, to maintain or restore the equilibrium in which the human organism can survive. Human beings are dangerously adventurous, sensitive, and vulnerable, and speaking can provide a delay, a calm, a controllable experience in the streaming of impulse and perception. Speaking gives a chance to size up the situation, recover initiative, and try out safely; it provides symbolic distance, abstraction, possibility, and hypothesis. Goldstein says,

> Words used as names are not simply tools which may be handled like concrete objects, but one means of detaching one from sense experience and helping one to organize the world in a conceptual way.

Emphasizing abstraction, Alfred Korzybski says a similar thing in neurological terms:

> Orientation by extension [by classification] induces an automatic delay of reactions which automatically stimulates the cortical region and regulates and protects the reactions of the usually over-stimulated thalamus.

(I don't know if there is any empirical demonstration of Korzybski's neurology. The psychology is improbable. My dark guess—it is a matter far beyond my competence —is that it is the delay or inhibition that induces the abstract classification, rather than the reverse. It is like an emergency computer being switched in when there is a threat of overheating, confusion, or other breakdown; and the auxiliary computer is programmed for the abstract language, a language of emergency and control rather than normal self-regulation. While I am at it, let me speculate further: The two-computer effect is physiologically the same as the interplay of the two hemispheres of the brain. Consider the following from *Speech and Brain-Mechanisms* by Wilder Penfield and Lamar Roberts:

> The ideational part of speech, whether spoken, heard, written, or read, depends upon the employment of a certain portion of one hemisphere alone—normally the left hemisphere. This location of a function in one hemisphere is, in itself, something new in mammalian evolution. Other intellectual functions, such as perception, the recording of current experiences, and the storing of generalizations or concepts in memory, are

made possible by the utilization of homologous areas of cerebral cortex on the two sides.

Then my dark guess is that normal speech is *always* a concrete coping with a real situation; the whole brain is in action; and the real situation may, of course, include remembered stored concepts as the second nature of speaker and hearer. But conceptualizing as such is an emergency function, activating only part of the brain.)

Not least, speech makes possible humor and irony, the perspective that helps us moderate the mischances and frustrations that we suffer.

An aphasic does not have these protections, cushioning, breathing space, ability to detach himself, arena of possibilities for trying out. (He may not be able to speak at all, may not be able to make abstract concepts, may not be able to relate concepts and his concrete experience, etc.) He is swept into an immediate response to stimulation and an all-out reaction to it—what Goldstein calls a "catastrophic reaction," the work of Korzybski's "the usually over-stimulated thalamus." Often an aphasic can say words, and in correct order, but they are not names or sentences saying a world that he believes. The lack, following on a lesion, is not "intellectual," for he may be able to reason in non-verbal ways; but he does not speak as a way of being in the world; he lacks a "symbolic attitude." Summarizing Hughlings Jackson, Head says,

> The general law underlying disturbances is that voluntary power is diminished, with retention of the power to carry on the same movement in a more automatic manner.

With our post-Freudian diffidence about volition, Goldstein prefers to say,

> Aphasic language . . . has changed from an active, spontaneous, productive means for expression of ideas

and feelings, to more passive reactions, utterance of stereotypes.

And elsewhere he puts it,

The aphasic is unable to emancipate himself from the world. . . . There is a shrinkage of his freedom.

Belief in one's assertions as expressing at least some reality is the condition of such emancipation as can be accomplished by words. As Kant pointed out long ago, in "The Refutation of Idealism," we spontaneously relate concept and experience in order to *have* a world. If one cannot do this, there is at once panic and paralysis.

In discussing aphasia, psychiatrists are usually reasoning from cases of brain damage. But in the previous chapter we saw that the paucity of speech alternatives of children in the culture of poverty has some of the same consequences: they become acutely embarrassed and burst into tears if the stereotype is not taken at face value; they diminish anxiety by an impulsive reaction and can become totally confused and lose all prudence; they quickly resort to punching, nudging, hand-stroking in lieu of speaking. These aphasic responses are not due to lack of mental development; rather, social conditions have obstructed and inhibited speaking, just as if there were a lesion with corresponding sequelae. Sensory deprivation, malnutrition, noise, too many social signals, distrust, excessive responsibility at too early an age, frustration of important simple goals because of lack of means and opportunity, these are positive causes; the inability to develop comes after the damage. And success in treatment, by removing or alleviating the causes, is better considered not as development but as more like the healing process of nature, which is very rapid and does not require long pedagogic exercises. The emphasis should not be pedagogic, but on removing traumatic conditions.

My intuition is that the obsessional man whom I described previously, who speaks with excruciating correctness, never modifying the common code to the situation or his purposes, is also aphasic. He does not *speak* the language, but handles words, as Goldstein says, like concrete objects. All his sentences are stereotypes from the dictionary and the manual of grammar; if they fail him, or if he gets a lively response, or if his impulsive needs are too strong for this rigid use of language, he will break down.

3

At the other extreme from aphasia is the pathology of living too much in the world of speech, in its excessive freedom as well as its empty verbalism. The formative power of speaking can be so unlimited that the sense of reality is deranged. Ideas and sentences crowd out experience. In paranoia the system of meanings is so tight that countervailing evidence counts for nothing. In what used to be called dementia, names are persons and formulas magically produce physical effects. Magic-speaking produces a world that is at first exciting, but finally static and unpragmatic, because there is a limit to the energy and novelty that can be squeezed out of words and dialectical possibilities. When everything can be made up, finally nothing is given, there are no facts.

The *prima facie* example of (non-committable) speech gone wild is religious superstition—what Freud called a shared psychosis. Because of the social validation and mutual support when everybody uses the same mad words, it is possible to persist in them without disaster—in fact, they have been the chief community bond (*religare*, "to bind") that mankind has been able to discover. Otto Rank said, "It may truly be said that words are gods, for gods are nothing but words." He cites Thoth and Khapera: "What flows from his mouth happens and what he speaks becomes. . . . I uttered my own name from my own mouth and forthwith I created myself." Similarly, said Rank, "Speech creates the soul."

In their enthusiasm to confute positivist linguists and cultural anthropologists, phenomenological and existentialist philosophers of language sometimes sound as if they too were out of their minds. I quoted Georges Gusdorf on how, by the network of words, man becomes master of the world. He says also, "The word creates the object, it creates personal existence. . . . To objects in the world correspond states of mind, the mere designation of which provides the resolution of internal ambiguities. . . . Speaking constitutes the essence of the world and the essence of man. Etc., etc." The only critique or corrective of experience, according to Gusdorf, is again verbal: "It is up to each person to assume the responsibility for his own language by searching for the *right* word." This is a fine thing to do, but we luckily also have other correctives, like facts and failures. Even Merleau-Ponty locks himself in the same box of panlogism:

> Speech, rather than like a means, is something like a substantial being [*être*], capable of containing things within it. . . . It gets to be like a universe. . . . Never does it cease, to leave room for pure meaning; it is never limited except by further language.

The first sentences are true, if we bear in mind that people usually also know that they are talking *about* things and that they have experience which is not verbal at all. But the last sentence is not true; speech is often stopped, and corrected, by dumb facts, animal feelings, silence.

Yet the enthusiasm of Gusdorf or Merleau-Ponty, who make human speech swallow up the world, is quite sane compared to the literal hypostasis of the Noösphere of Teilhard de Chardin: This computer of the universal code is supposed to be a biologically emergent incarnate spirit and a proper object of our love. We shall see later (Chapter X) that, if only for technological reasons, the people in Communications theory tend to get carried away into *this* kind of excess. Whereas, for the philosophers, human speech swallows up the whole world, the scientists want communication to occur without human speakers altogether.

In this book, in which I try to describe how people actually speak and the language that is actually spoken, I find that I am steering a middle course between the dogmatic phenomenologists on the one hand and the dogmatic linguists and scientists on the other. This gives me the genuine pleasure of being able to affirm platitudes that all the authors are denying.

In a previous discussion I mentioned a range of cases of speech abused, e.g. speaking instead of acting as the conclusion of a practical syllogism, and I sketched a scale of withdrawal from life into words, with corresponding weakening of language. We now see that people are able to use these self-deluding devices because they feel that just by speaking they *are* doing what is real and important. Yet the more they just speak, the worse they speak. It is with speech as with the fine arts. An artist must believe in his medium, that it says something, it adds to meaning and does not just copy; and so he is impelled to use it abstractly, to bring out *its* meaning. But then soon, when he tries to express only the medium, without his own action or passion and without nature, the product is increasingly thin.

But there is no semantical rule to tell at what point speaking ceases to be functional and begins to be so self-contained as to defeat function. At what point does a theological sentence, which was useful to reconcile a soul to something too astounding or absurd in existence, turn into a superstition? At what point does the freedom of hypothesis that is necessary for science become speculation that does not take empirical facts seriously? At what point does political rhetoric cease to clarify issues, hearten one's partisans, and persuade new partisans, and become the sloganeering that increases fanaticism and prevents either reconciliation or reform or revolutionary reconstruction? We have all heard speakers so lost in their self-naming languages that they seem to be blind or mad. But it is often a matter of a slight historical shift—in politics it may be a matter of a few weeks, in a personal quarrel or love affair it may be a matter of a few moments—for effective speech to turn into self-mesmerizing speech.

"What is honour? a word," says Falstaff. "What is that word honour? air." The conception of honor when Shakespere wrote this, and already by the time that Falstaff was supposed to have said it, had worn down to be celebrity, prestige. The fat knight was intelligent not to risk an arm or a leg for it, nor to end up dead like Walter Blunt. Yet there had been a time when honor meant the chivalric fealty, the personal commitment and loyalty and being known for that, that was the effective ideology of the feudal system. And in the still more distant past, it had been truer than ideology; the bands of horsemen did stick together by personal allegiance to the chief, as we have seen it in our time among guerilla bands loyal to Makhno in the Ukraine or to Che Guevara in Bolivia. One would not call such honor "air."

By the end of the sixteenth century, when *Henry IV* was written—and Cervantes was writing *Don Quixote*—the old feudalism was dead and gone, along with Richard II's lovely rhetoric and the separatist local speech of Hotspur and Owen Glendower. Henry Hereford and the

Tudors have the support of new classes—city folk, merchants, freehold yeomen and squires. And honor has become air.

Yet in the same Histories, Shakespere tried to give the word "honour" a new lease on life, as national patriotism, for instance in Henry V's speech on Crispin's Day at Agincourt. Honor was now securely fastened to the ideology of dying for England and being a household word in every English mouth. It is likely that Shakespere himself believed in the renewed word—at least he consigns Falstaff to disgrace—and patriotic honor certainly proved to have vitality and reality for the nation-states for a couple of centuries.

But four hundred years have now passed. And Falstaff seems to have the right of it. Fat Falstaff was undoubtedly the most esthetically realized of all the characters in the Histories, *therefore* he is the most philosophical; he speaks in the universal voice. Shakespere must have known it all along!—even if he deceived himself. "What is honour? the same old baloney."

Let me summarize the argument of this chapter. I seem to be making a point in semantics: that there is a difference between words as signs that help us to cope with their designates and words whose designation has been blurred, so they become detached from experience and we expend ourselves in the words. But it is the nature of speaking a language that these two cannot be clearly distinguished in actual speaking. We cannot use words to cope unless we believe in their meaning and assert it, and this belief depends on utterance, grammar, history, the existence of speakers and hearers. Conversely, we cannot finally describe a language, its pronunciation, grammar, and meaning of words, unless we take into account its uses in speaking, including the peculiar difficulty explored in this chapter.

CHAPTER VI

Some Reflections on Scientific Linguistics

Again and again I find myself dissenting from the main line of the scientific linguists of the past fifty years—the anthropologists, the positivists, and the structuralists. (The authors I mean are Sapir, Whorf, Saussure, Leonard Bloomfield, Louis Hjelmslev, Zellig Harris, Jakobson, Chomsky, Vygotsky.) It seems to me that in abstracting language from speaking and hearing in actual situations, they make three fundamental, and connected, mistakes: (1) They exaggerate constancy and supra-individuality as against the variability and interpersonality of natural language; the "language" that they discuss, with its constant forms and self-contained rules, is sometimes an artifact of their method of investigation. (2) They say that the forms of language can rarely, if ever, be explained by meanings in experience and practical use, and the forms themselves do not have meaning. (3) They have a disposition to treat language and communication as a calculus of forms and a processing of information that could dispense with human speakers and hearers altogether.

Yet they are earnest scholars—I am not a scholar in the field at all—and possibly I miss their point. So for a few pages let me reflect on why they do what they do and how it seems to me.

1

The linguist [says Bloomfield] studies the language of all persons alike. The individual features in which [a use of] language differs from the ordinary speech of the time and place interest the linguist . . . much less than do the features that are common to all speakers.

This is Saussure's distinction between *parole* (speech) and *langue* (language). Why this emphasis? It makes immense sense for an utterly foreign anthropologist trying to record an obscure Amerindian language, where it is hard enough to pin down the code without the complication of individual variations—and this *was* one of Bloomfield's chief concerns. It makes sense, though less sense, for a student of any foreign language, trying to get started on real conversation and reading. But for a native speaker, the only reasonable sense of "language" is how he copes verbally with actual situations, for *his* purposes, not purposes of recording; and in such language, variability, including frequent innovation, is of the essence. The interesting *reality* for a linguist would be what speakers do to the code that they have inherited in common, which is, indeed, largely an assumed entity, never spoken.

But, it is argued, this assumed code must exist in a fairly precise, constant form, otherwise how can the hearer understand, how can the speakers communicate? This argument takes the hearer as a passive receptor rather than an active interpreter and participant. Rather, to be catching the particular drift of the discourse and the variations from the routine code is essential for hearing; the "correct" has less message. And the speakers *do* rather precisely understand the circumstances in which their speech is coping—its setting, social class, feeling tone, personalities, immediate purposes, underlying intentions. It is only the outside observer or recorder who might find these circumstances too vague, and for a sensitive observer they are often not so vague as all that. It is continually argued by the linguist that the meanings and the circumstances are not precise enough to be part of a "scientific" description, whereas the sounds and grammatical forms can be pinned down precisely; but even if this were true—which it often is not—what is the point of "science" which does not clarify what is really going on?

The method of investigation during much of these fifty years has been likely to produce an artifact which then becomes the basis of theory. The linguists have set store by pair tests, in which a native speaker is asked to try two closely related sounds or forms and decide if the difference makes a difference—a difference in meaning or, in more sophisticated method, just a "different word." Or a speaker is asked which expressions presented to him are idiomatic. But recently, Labov and others have shown that such speech-for-a-test is not the same as spontaneous speech for real use; nor is it very competent (just as testing a child in school does not evoke what he knows and does on the playground in his own style for his own interests).[1] In real use,

1. The inferiority of self-monitored speech is exactly analogous to the result of Ralph Hefferline's experiment: The subject is subjected to a recurring annoying stimulus which he can diminish and obliterate if he makes a certain subtle squirm of his body. He does this less efficiently if he is told how to do it than if he is left in ignorance and comes to it by spontaneous motions.

caught on the fly by a microphone, there is less homogeneity of sound and form and far more subtle adaptation to rates of speed, passions, social classes, formality of occasion, etc. Yet the hearer adjusts without difficulty. We understand a friend who has a stuffed nose. I hear the Puerto Rican taxi driver say "seedy," and I understand "city." Careless and creole pronunciations and usages are in fact far more common than standard ones are, yet we freely communicate. The freedom to vary the phonemes is certainly not zero, as Jakobson claimed. Thus, the protocols for an elaborate, accurate, positivistic structure of language, e.g. Zellig Harris's ,*Structural Linguistics,* might themselves be grossly unscientific.

But not only is the speech tested and self-monitored, but, in sophisticated method, the test itself is a Chinese puzzle. Consider the following, from Chomsky's *Syntactic Structures,* explaining how to determine phonemic distinctions without asking for meaning or taking context into account:

> A careful field worker would probably use the pair test, either with two informants or with an informant and a tape recorder. He might make a random sequence of copies of the utterance tokens that interest him and then determine whether or not the speaker can consistently identify them. If there is a consistent identification, the linguist may apply an even stricter test, asking the speaker to repeat each sound several times, and running the pair test over again on the repetitions. . . . The operational tests for linguistic notions may require the informant to respond, but *not* [italics, P.G.] to express his opinions about his behavior, his judgment about synonymy, about phonemic distinctness, etc. The informant's opinions may be based on all sorts of irrelevant factors. This is an important distinction that must be carefully observed if the operational basis for grammar is not to be trivialized.

This is extraordinary. Why should the man's opinion on what is a "word" be any more reliable than on things he might know something about? It is like testing a rat's intelligence in a sterile maze rather than in the odorous wall where he is at home. We saw above that telegraphers find it hard even to *hear* a random sequence of utterances without context. For a man who uses language to speak, to make a rule that he must not talk of the meaning is like telling him that he can think of anything but a pink elephant. Psychologically, if a man is restricted to saying nothing except whether or not he can distinguish certain sounds as parts of "words" in the abstract, his answers will soon be about sounds as such—no different than the Seashore test for discrimination of musical pitches; they will tell us nothing whatever about whether those sounds are part of his language.

An informant who was not browbeaten might likely say, "That depends. That depends. Are 'where' and 'wear' different?—depends on how I got outta bed. When I talk to Harry, 'nothin' and 'nothing' are the same; when I talk to you they're not."

It is a high scientific price to pay, maybe warping the data, just to stick to a method of explanation.

If I am asked if a sentence is grammatical or idiomatic, I often find it quite impossible to answer without considerable speculation about its meaning in possible contexts. My immediate spontaneous judgment of an isolated sentence is not reliable.

2

To accept definitions of meaning, which at best are makeshifts, in place of identification in formal terms, is to abandon scientific discourse.

The methodical error which has held back our work is our habit of putting the question in terms of meaning and not of form.

Bloomfield urges us to exclude meaning from explaining form on every third page of his *Language*. One important reason, surely, is to get the simple constant code, for meanings in their contexts are infinitely diverse. And for these linguists—though not for the speakers themselves—they are not accurately knowable or are even unknowable. But in my opinion, most meanings in context *are* roughly knowable, and it is impossible for *any* behavioral science to be as precise as scientific linguistics pretends. The precision is bought at the price of artificiality.

But there is a converse reason to exclude meaning from influencing form, which would seem to be more cogent, though I have not seen it spelled out anywhere. If the code itself is not pure of meaning, then it cannot be a good instrument of communication, since *its* meanings would interfere with the information to be conveyed. Ideally, in this view, language would be like a good telephone and the stimulated message would be wordless. But for speakers, and for many other people much of the time, there are no such wordless meanings, unverbalized experiences. It is only in life situations when we are not about to speak that we know wordless meanings, and then often with great difficulty. And I shall argue shortly that the forms, the "instrument," are full of meanings, vague or sharp. Then when actual sentences are spoken and understood, I prefer to say that they are not an instrument of communication between speaker and listener, they *are* their communication, the structure of their interaction, coping with the needs of the situation so far as it can be done by speech. Sentences do not point to meanings or stimulate meanings; the meanings are explicit in the spoken and understood sentences.

There is a more modest reason, a reason of scientific style, to try to exclude meaning as much as possible in explaining forms. This is the "neo-grammarian" impulse to stick close to the surface data in the smallest compass, to explain as many phenomena as possible by a purely linguistic law, and then to collect the exceptions and try to find some other purely linguistic law. (This was the method that worked so spectacularly in classical philology, e.g. Werner's Law adding to and refining Grimm's Law.) Most essential is not to seek for explanations in vague propositions of psychology and metaphysics. With this parsimonious method, I am in full sympathy. As a literary critic I like to stick close to the text and show that it is coherent (or falls apart) in its own terms, without bringing in history or biography, not to speak of metapsychology and cosmic myths. Thus, when our speaker says, "Nothin," but does not say, "swinnin," but "swingin," I am quite satisfied with a simple phonetic explanation, such as: He tends to shorten the terminal unaccented syllable but not the *ng* in "swing," especially since it's only a morpheme that he skimps! (I have no doubt that this satisfying explanation is not quite correct; it's made up out of my hat.)

But parsimony is an heuristic principle and not a dogma. Sometimes other explanations are *prima facie,* and then it is ridiculous not to draw on common experience, common behavior, the facts of life, well-known history, documentable accidents, etc.; e.g. in explaining a play of Shakespere, it would be absurd to refuse to mention the architecture of the Globe, the social composition of the audience, the politics of Elizabeth, the source in Holinshed. And in linguistics it is hardly far-fetched to bring in the meaning in context, what needs to be said, since this is indeed why people speak.

In rejecting the influence of meaning, linguists come on as if they were attacking a kind of Lamarckianism—the

inheritance (in the code) of acquired adaptive characteristics (= meaningful modifications in actual speech situations). Rather, they believe that the social code is entirely
determined by its genetic inheritance of mutations and
natural selection (= neo-grammarian laws), which never
were adaptive. But the analogy is not exact. Language is
behavior. There is not a germ plasm and a somatoplasm.
And it is obvious that innumerable forms have come to be
because of reasons of meaning, e.g. abstract words formed
from concrete actions—"concept" is formed from a word
for grasping, "abstract" from dragging, "comprehend"
from taking hold.

To explain my own view, let me spread a spectrum of
cases, going from meaning-not-influencing-form to mean-
ing-influencing-form:

At one extreme is obvious dissonance of meaning and
form: *Fräulein,* a young lady, in the neuter gender; *nauta,*
a male sailor, in the feminine declension.

Very many meanings have little relation to the form
they fill: "The cow has two horns"; "The American government has three branches." Both these sentences have
a subject, verb, and object in that order; but it is suffi-
ciently explained, I think, by Bloomfield's remark that this
is one of the two "favorite forms" of English sentences (the
other "favorite form" being the imperative).

In many other cases, however, the need to single out or
to emphasize does influence the word order and construction: "The wrench is what I want, not the pliers."

We say, "big black horse" and never "black big horse,"
and no obvious meaning is expressed by the order, any
more than by the rule in French that polysyllabic adjectives follow the noun. But we can say either "Who is
this blonde little girl?" or "Who is this little blonde girl?"
and there is a difference in nuance in the two situations.

Here is a case of phonetics that allows for alternative

explanations: We say, "You're lazy," eliding the *a* in "are," but we cannot drop it in "You *are* lazy." More interestingly, in Black English the copula is dropped entirely in "He lazy," but it must be borrowed back from Standard English in "He *is* lazy." Is this simply for the phonetic reason that the emphasis prevents the elision or, as the Black dialect seems to bear out, is it the underlying meaning of the verb reasserting itself?

Here is a fairly unambiguous case in grammar: We can say, in the imperfect, "He was breaking the ground when she came" or "He was cutting the grass when she came"; but it is odd to say, "He was breaking the window when she came" or "He was cutting his finger when she came." In the latter sentences, the imperfect doesn't make sense.[2] Naturally there is no difficulty, for purposes of methodological purity, in setting up a grammatical category—with a list—excluding the imperfect past of transitive verbs of actions that occur quick and once and for all. I again think that this is too high a price to pay for consistency.

I tried out "He was breaking the window" and "He was cutting his finger" on my seven-year-old, and she burst out laughing and said "That's a stupid sentence!" That is, she not only made all the derivations to the imperfect with the competence that Chomsky so rightly praises and wonders at,[3] but she also, *in the very same action,* derived a semantical proposition: the contradiction of the grammar and common experience. And every parent knows that children of this age are acutely sensitive to sarcasm, which

2. My editor at Random House offers: "The burglar was carefully breaking the window when the police arrived."

3. "It must be admitted that the ability of a human being to do this far surpasses our present understanding. . . . The young child has succeeded in carrying out what from the formal point of view seems to be a remarkable type of theory construction. Furthermore, this task is accomplished in an astonishingly short time, etc." (from Chomsky's review of Skinner).

also depends on the clash between meaning and form, though they do not yet much understand irony, where the clash is more between meanings. Children's power of language extends indifferently, in the same act, to deductions of form and meaning; it does not recognize the distinction made so sharp by the structural linguists.

Finally, here is an interesting nuance that goes to the heart of language, the relation of speaker and hearer: We can say, "I am walking too fast," "You are walking too fast," "He is walking too fast." We can say, "I admire the view," "I wonder what they're doing," "I'm surprised at you," and "He admires the view," "He wonders what they're doing," "He's surprised at her." But there's something wrong in saying, "You admire the view," "You wonder what they're doing," "You're surprised at me"—we would have to add or imply "You admire the view, don't you?" "I see you wonder what they're doing," "(I guess) you're surprised at me." Otherwise the hearer might say, "Stop telling me what I'm feeling." On the other hand, "inner" actions that are likely to involve obvious overt behavior *are* allowable in the second person: "You love her," "You hate me," "You're afraid of him"—the hearer might protest that it's not so, but he won't object to our *saying* so. The nuance here is definite and quite remarkable. It may be that *mens naturaliter Platonica,* but speaking people seem to be naturally behaviorists when they confront each other. In cases like this, unbehavioristic sentences become unidiomatic.

Now what balanced judgment can we make from this little spectrum of cases? It includes cases of sound, grammar, word order, construction, and syntax. The cases are not trivial, and they are fairly *prima facie.* But the only ones that are extremely common are the change of word order and choice of construction to emphasize meaning, and the linguists would call these matters of style, not language. I collected the cases without difficulty and without research (there are certainly much stronger examples that could be given), but I did have to seek for them—most sentences that occur are not apt examples.

In my judgment, the truth about form and meaning is as follows: In the majority of sentences, the meaning—what needs to be said—and the usual variants of the language are well enough adjusted so that no problem of form and meaning arises. In good colloquial and literary speech the code is continually modified in the direction of saying what needs to be said, but the modification is not so drastic as to call attention to itself, and it is just for the occasion. Yet, in a large number of steady cases, like those we have been discussing, the meanings do influence the forms and determine what is idiomatic and etiquette. In brief, people will generally speak in the usual way, just as they do other things, so long as it says their say well enough. But they will always select conventional formal elements and sharpen vaguely meaningful formal elements in the direction of making sense. And they will be anomalous on the infrequent occasions that *that* is necessary to make sense.

To put it another way: There is no distinction between language and style, but most people most of the time speak a fairly standard style. Standard style is the subject of linguistics.

Or to put it still another way: Meaning determines form, but the limit is not the sky. The speaker is severely restricted by the expectation of the hearer. "His" meaning—what needs to be said—is very much determined by what is conceivable and what is etiquette in his speech community. The subject of linguistics is: the relation, often tension, between what needs to be said in the situation and the social code, and the relation, often tension, between the saying of the speaker and the hearing of the hearer.

Let me at once make clear what I do *not* mean. "What needs to be said" is not the thoughts or intentions of the speaker; it is the situation of the speaker and hearer as a problem to be coped with. An important purpose of the anti-semantic posture of the linguists of the past fifty years has been to reject "mentalism," as Bloomfield called it, and I agree with this. Throughout the previous century, language was defined in "mental" terms. For instance, in 1875 William Whitney began *The Life and Growth of Language* with

> Language may be briefly and comprehensively defined as the means of expression of human thought.

And in 1930 Louis Gray, in *The Foundations of Language,* was still saying,

> Generally speaking, the function of language is the conveyance of thought. . . . It is the means of expressing emotional and mental concepts and of communicating them to other living beings.

But language is too communal and public to be made to depend on what goes on inside people's heads. In each individual it is habitual and spontaneous; there probably are usually no "thoughts" at all. And I agree with the behaviorist thesis that mental states are too impenetrable for science and we can generally get precise clues from overt behavior.

Meaning is not mental. It is a characteristic of most overt animal behavior. It is the unifying tendency in the on-going situation, the coping.

In my opinion, the profound error that the scientific linguists have made has been to retain words like *"instrument* of communication" and *"means* of expression" from the old definitions. Then they isolate language and describe it like a mechanism, as if it were a telephone. But the message is explicit in the language. Speaking a language is not just signaling; it is the human way of being in the world with the others; it *is* communication.

3

Although Bloomfield insisted that we must not use meaning to explain form, he was by no means willing to say the converse—that form does not have meaning. On the contrary, he not only pointed out what is obvious—that grammatical forms have empirical meaning (e.g. when a speaker puts an *s* on a noun, he is talking about more than one actual thing; when he puts *ed* on a verb, he is placing the event with reference to his own actual time as a speaker)—but he also made the broader claim that language *shapes* meaning—its forms determine how the speakers take their experience:

> One could say that every utterance of a speech-form involves a minute semantic innovation.

> Since every practical situation is in reality unprecedented, the apt response of a good speaker may always border on semantic innovation. Both the wit and the poet often cross this border, and their innovations may become popular.

Essentially, Bloomfield was an old-fashioned philologist, a lover of language, sensitive to its power. In his opening gambit in *Language,* we saw, he said that language was "trivial and unimportant" except for its non-verbal consequences, but he was just kidding.

But the positivists and structuralists go the whole hog: Meaning does not influence form; form has no meaning. Language is a meaningless instrument for conveying meaning. Chomsky says,

The notion of "structural meaning" appears to be quite suspect. It is questionable that the grammatical devices available in language are used consistently enough so that meaning can be assigned to them directly.

This remark baffles me. Doesn't *Noun + s* rather consistently *mean* more than one? or *will + Verb* mean a time future to the speaker's present? or *if + Imperfect Subjunctive* mean that the fact isn't so? Doesn't the word order tell us whether Tom beat Dick or Dick beat Tom? Etc., etc. Statistically these meanings are *consistent* enough, though there may be exceptions, as in other behavior. To be sure, the meanings conveyed by grammar are usually quite broad, but that is their value: It is by them that a listener catches the drift of what is being communicated, so he can follow it; and the grammar keeps *naming* the broad aspects for him—what is being talked about, when, from what point of view, with what attitude, and so forth. If the grammar said nothing substantive, communication would be incredibly difficult and slow. (In general, I agree with Skinner, Labov, Bailey, and others that we get a more realistic notion of what is happening in speech if we consider it from the point of view of the hearer rather than the speaker.)

Hjelmslev, the most philosophical of the positivists, goes further. Chomsky offers to give us the "simplest grammar of English," but Hjelmslev says,

> The linguistic theoretician . . . sets up a general calculus in which all conceivable cases are foreseen. This calculus is deduced from his definitions independently of all experience. Linguistic theory cannot be verified by reference to existing texts and languages.[4]

The model for this kind of linguistics is the positivistic

4. Incidentally, I have a lot of respect for this kind of musico-mathematical enterprise. It is often beautiful in itself, and it sometimes does cast light on real things.

symbolic logic that was in its full morning when Hjelmslev wrote (1928). Meaning does not influence form, just as empirical sentences tell us nothing about "analytic" sentences and the validity of inferences. Form has no meaning, just as logical sentences must be kept pure of empirical reference.

In linguistics, the effect of totally separating form from meaning is to dispense with human speakers altogether, at least in theory, and this has been the tendency of the positivists. But this tendency was apparently sharply reversed by Noam Chomsky when he showed that we cannot explain how people make indefinitely numerous new grammatical combinations unless we assume that they have a faculty to do it that belongs to them as individuals. He is especially impressed by the speech of children, since they have heard only a limited number of sentences to imitate and so must be generating the variations by themselves:

> The fact that all normal children acquire . . . grammars of great complexity with remarkable rapidity suggests that human beings are somehow especially designed to do this, with data-handling or "hypothesis-formulating" ability of unknown character and complexity.

And it *is* remarkable how five-year-olds can accurately distinguish and *say* that something is possible, probable, pretty sure, rather likely, rather unlikely, doubtful, etc., just as it is remarkable that they can distinguish and *act out* playing, pretending, making believe, acting as if, mimicking, fantasying, and lying. Totally absorbed in the game, they go through the motions that pebbles are breakfast rolls, but they do not try to chew them.

Nevertheless, for some reason that defeats me, Chomsky insists on restricting this rational faculty to operating on strings of sentences, spinning out an algebra, rather than taking it, as Kant does, as part of the total intellectual power of people that gives form to all their experience so they can have it *as* experience. It is as if, in explaining the leaps of a cat, Chomsky showed—as is the case—that the cat makes accurate practical judgments of space, time, gravity, and energy, and then he concluded that a cat is a born geometer and theorist of dynamics. Wouldn't it be less strange to try to explain the leaps in terms of the cat's entire biological experience, his sensory and motor apparatus, his appetites—the meanings of the situation? The subtile intellectual powers of a child in speaking are neither more nor less precise than in learning to run across a stony field or to throw and catch a ball. In my opinion, they are the same formative powers; Kant spelled them out in detail and combined them as the "synthetic unity of apperception"—what we in our times would call "Gestalt-forming." The ability is complex, but its character is not all that unknown.

When we are attentive, we structure all our blind perceptions to become experience, parts of meaningful situations; otherwise the intellect would be biologically useless to us in coping with the continual novelty of the environment. It is not necessary for the intellect to have preformed counters to work on, like "words" or the counters of a game of chess or checkers. We make the sounds into words as part of the same formative act as we combine the words into grammatical sentences.

Go back to the seven-year-old who bursts out laughing and says that "He was cutting his finger" is a stupid sentence. According to Chomsky she has no right to say this; she is making a two-fold mistake: She has assigned meaning to the imperfect past tense—but form has no meaning—and she is laughing at the dissonance between the meaning of the tense and her experience of cutting fingers—but experience is irrelevant to form. In fact, however, she does do all this in one uninterrupted arc.

In constructing their languages, the structuralists proceed by levels: the phonemes, the words, the morphemes, the grammar, the syntax, and only then the semantics, the application to meaningful situations. This is a convenient method of exposition, and grammarians have always used it. But it is far-fetched to take it as the nature of things, as if, in learning to speak, children first made sounds, then letters, then monosyllables, then polysyllables, then words, then sentences, and then applied them. But children do it all at once, making meaningful sentences. They do not proceed from the simple to the complex but—at least *from the adult hearer's point of view*—from the more confused and undiscriminating to the sharper and more discriminating. The linguists here make the same error as the logicians, who start from the particulars and go to classes and then to propositional functions and then to assertions about reality. But every experience contains the given and the universal, content and structure, and the possibility of truth or error.

Chomsky assigns to his speakers the rationality of disembodied spirits made of words. In the pair test, we saw, he forbids the informant to make any discrimination except to answer the question, "Is this a different word?" And the objects of "data-handling" and "hypothesis-formulating" are restricted to forms of sentences. I am puzzled why a computer, programmed to allow for certain random choices, could not spin out new sentences from the counters, since the sentences do not have to cope with any actual situation.

The cultural anthropologists, we have seen, explain away the speakers by another route—by making the code rigidly determine what a speaker *can* say and the pattern of culture rigidly determine what he *can* mean. Then the

drama of speech, the tension between form and meaning,
vanishes. I don't know about primitive cultures, but in
the culture I am used to there is no such rigid patterning
by the code. The determinism is about on a par with
etiquette and dress, rather less than consumption habits or
sexual taboos, much less than death rites or obedience to
officers. Indeed, in a high technological urban society,
speech is, comparatively, one of the areas of freedom.

Those who are interested in perfecting communications
technology, e.g. the telephone company, readily scuttle
natural pronunciation and colloquial expression for efficiency in sending and receiving the message. The odd
dialect of the astronauts has been built from traditions of
the armed services, but fundamentally it must be efficient
for space suits—"Roger. I read you. Over." Also, much of
structural linguistics looks like an effort to devise a trans-
lating machine, and the linguists do not care about the
nuances of idiomatic language.

Finally, with the scholarly Theory of Communications,
e.g. cybernetics, meaning itself is defined as pattern, and
communication is the exchange of patterns or bits of information, so that there is no need for human speakers and
hearers altogether. (I discuss this in Chapter XI.) Thus we
come full circle. We start with meanings explicit in the
forms of language to cope with human situations. The
linguists separate form and meaning, studying form in
linguistics and leaving meaning to the non-linguistic behavior of the speakers. The Theory of Communications
takes over meaning too and dispenses with the speakers.

Part 2

LITERATURE

CHAPTER VII

Constructed
Languages

We can take the study of language as one of the humanities or as one of the social sciences. In either case, its concern is good language—there is no "value-neutral" social science. Such different students as Jespersen, Sapir, and Bloomfield conclude their essays on *Language* with paragraphs on the progress of language. Much of recent work by positivists, General Semanticists, and theorists of Communications has been aimed toward the prophylaxis of language—to clean it up—and the efficiency of language—to carry messages without redundancy and noise. Humanists and pedagogues have always tried to make language more expressive. We have noticed, in this book, that the world of words, in which all human beings inevitably live, is rife with delusion. And the social critics of our time —Orwell is the foremost example among many—have talked about the degeneration of language in modern conditions, just as Confucius said that the first step in political reform was to rectify the names.

In principle there seem to be three possibilities: to improve the people who speak, who then will speak better; to take language as it is and use it better; or to reform the common code and make rules to prevent its abuse.

No doubt, the forthright way to improve language is to improve the political and social institutions and the general moral culture. If there were different, and less, administration, there would be less administrative double-talk. If people were free and competent in their communities and jobs, they would be immune to demagogic rhetoric. If there were not so many ads, children would take words more seriously. If the young didn't go to school so much, some of them might learn to read English. In preceding chapters I have given examples of psychopathological conditions that confuse and weaken speech.

Less effective, but maybe sometimes effective, is the influence of oral or written literature, which I would define as deliberately improved common speech. Where colloquial speech is good, it is a source for literature, as Wordsworth said he used country speech. It is a traditional opinion that a chief use of literature is to improve the language of the tribe. It has been claimed that reading the Bible made people talk better. Matthew Arnold piously believed that literature, "the best that has been thought and said," was good for the readers' "conduct of life." And literature does demonstrably renovate at least the public language; compare Dryden and the journalism after him, or the American realists and the journalism after them.

But I am much more dubious about programs to improve language by drastically reconstructing it and making prophylactic rules, and in this chapter I will criticize a couple of such programs. So far as I know, they have never caught on. There are good reasons why they don't—and I am not sure they ought to.

1 . Positivist Languages

The strategy of positivism is to clean up language and try to prevent further contamination once and for all. The only allowable words are names of objects whose existence is empirically verifiable and auxiliary formal words that have no meaning in themselves. There are strict grammatical rules for the organization of these names and words into sentences: to give a simple example, in Russell's language, the name for a quality like "yellow" can be said of only one name for a thing, but the name for a relation like "to the right of" must be said of two or more names of things connected by the relation. Finally, there are explicit rules for the combination of correct sentences into inferences and arguments.

At their strictest, positivist languages do not allow the sentences and inferences to be referred to experience for confirmation—that is, they are nominalist in the tradition of William Ockham. Reasoning is about the names and their combination. Recourse to experience is allowed only to correct a name or propose another. Philosophical questions of necessity, contingency, meaning, and so forth are questions of whether or not the names have been correctly applied and combined. Thus speech is controllable from the beginning to the end; it can be checked and corrected by a definite procedure with a limited set of counters.

Also—in the tradition of Hume—the grammatical and logical rules are conventional; they are made up and agreed on by the speakers. The usual metaphor is that language is a game, with made-up rules that one can change if it is convenient. Since it is felt that traditional language has only the warrant of custom and is vague, mystifying, and often self-contradictory, it is reasonable to change the custom for prophylaxis or for reasons of elegance or utility.

Laymen always find such a language pointless and oppressive. Forgetting that natural language is conventional through and through, they judge the rules to be "arbitrary"; and forgetting that they themselves live in a world of words, they judge the nominalism to be "unreal." But in my opinion, such a self-contained conventional nominalism is like a breath of fresh air, at least at first. Far from being arid and pedantic, it springs directly from the free action and rule-giving that belongs to speech. It makes speech like music and mathematics. And of course, an important purpose of contemporary positivist language, following Russell's symbolic logic, is to identify logic and mathematics.

Even as literature, the freedom and autonomy pay off in very stylish moments. There is a teasing cubism to Russell's definition of cardinal number as "the class of all classes similar to a given class." [1] It is a witty and profound observation that "any sentence whatever follows from a contradictory sentence." Logicians come to this by setting up certain rules of inference; but it is true of language in general that, if speech does not distinguish and exclude, we can say anything. In the glossary of *The Structure of Literature,* written under the influence of Carnap, I am able to define Character as "the part of the beginning that persists as a source of probability" and Passion as "the disintegration of character": thus, when Oedipus loses his bearings, he says, "Happen whatever! I am the child of Chance!"—the formal or neo-grammarian way of explaining helps us see how the poet puts it together.

1. The clue is the one-one match that can be made between the members of all classes with the same number of members, no matter what the things are.

Needless to say, a positivist reformer like Carnap is not after freedom of expression or musical style. He wants to avoid error by grounding speech in empirical knowledge, specifically physical science—his language is "physicalist"; he means to be anti-metaphysical and behaviorist in psychology. Therefore, besides a formal language (*The Logical Syntax of Language*), he provides us, in *Testability and Meaning,* with a method for tying down the names to simple physical objects of ordinary experience. We introduce a new name in terms of the laboratory operations and observations that test for the substance. Thus, instead of defining a chemical compound in terms of chemical theory, we mention the familiar laboratory things like Bunsen burner, scales, water, test-tube, table, and correspondingly familiar actions like pouring, putting, reading a pointer, and say that if the results are such and such we will call it so and so. This is excellent vernacular speech; it is concrete and it flows from what actually goes on. (I single out Carnap in this discussion because he was one of my teachers, though I was not very receptive.)

It happens, however, that Auguste Comte, the first great champion of positivist empiricism, would have required an entirely different set of familiar objects and their primitive names to give language a solid foundation, namely: village, neighborhood, home, man, woman, child, mother, speech, authority, and other facts of sociology. And the syntax necessary to combine the names of these things would not be the same as to combine spatial relations, inanimate objects, and pointer readings. Yet social facts are perhaps the most familiar of any facts, and they are certainly as much efficient and material causes as any. For Comte, artifacts like laboratories and laboratory equipment would come far down on the list of objects to introduce into language and reasoning; there would first have to be division of labor, profession, discipline. For a

Marxist sociologist, they might have to wait upon the analysis of social class, market, ideology, which also leap to the eye in historical situations, and there are no real non-historical situations.

It would make no difference where we start in building a language if indeed the physicalist and sociological languages were complete, so one could make a one-one swap of their sentences. But that is not how it is, and it won't be so in any foreseeable future. At present it is also unlikely that researchers in very different branches of knowledge could efficiently use the same syntax, or would choose to—except factitiously, which is a disaster, as when the social sciences ape the mathematical style of the physical sciences. (Aristotle pointed out that it is the sign of an ignorant man to be more precise than is possible.) On the other hand, if it is agreed that each branch uses its own positivist language, we have to renounce the Baconian ideal of a universal organon of language and method, with guaranteed harmonious progress step by step.

I have found it hard to explore these problems with a positivist. Since he is certain what is basic matter-of-fact, he knows the best language to say it, and he at once puts my difficulty in his language. If I don't want to put it that way, his eyes glaze over. If, for the sake of argument, I do put it in his terms, soon *I* become impatient, for his terms are not saying what I think I mean, and they get further and further away from what bothers me. The usual way by which we try to understand one another, by modifying our rough common language, has been foreclosed. Anyway, he is convinced that my error is, as he would say, "psychological," since I question what is to him quite plain. Maybe it is. But he doesn't use psychotherapeutic means to make me see the light.

There is a similar impasse in discussing the semantical relation, the relation of a sign and its designate. I ask a

General Semanticist, "What is this sound 'table' that you keep saying?" He repeats "Table!" and he points to the table. I say, "Oh, finger!" "No!!" "Index finger?" He sticks a label "Table" onto the table. I say, unbelieving, "Scotch tape? . . . Aha! set of commodities of Western Imperialism!" Of course, I am just playing fun-and-games. I do know what a table is and what it is called. Nevertheless, I am not fooling. Since in the end I will not and cannot speak language as he wants, with such a sharp distinction between name and thing, I might as well pick a fight to begin with.

In order to get back to what is too simple to question, a desperate recourse of positivist languages has been to revert to Berkeley and attach the basic names to percepts— the Lockean "ideas." These are absolutely certain: "red patch," "sound of middle C," "seeing the pointer at 7:32 A.M." This was more or less the tack of the Vienna Circle, in the manner of Ernst Mach, before Carnap and others developed the physicalist language. But it is desperate, because sensation-sentences cannot be publicly verified without complicated behavioristic interpretation, including verbal reports, and a language built up from atomic perception-sentences would be bewilderingly complicated.

In my opinion, a far more accurate positivist language grounded in brute primary experience could be drawn from Gestalt psychology and phenomenology, but it would look mighty strange. "Here," "now," and "here now" would be not adverbs but a kind of super-proper nouns. "You" and "I" would be not pronouns but a kind of verbal operators actively organizing experience into figures-and-grounds. We saw in the previous chapter that "You" cannot occur in sentences unknowable to "I." We would not take the moods of sentences as indicative, optative, imperative, etc., but rather as how the speakers are actually contacting the environment. In *Gestalt Therapy* I divided the process of contacting the environment into the stages of Fore-Contact, Contact, Identification, and Assimilation. And we might add Dewey's On-Goingness and End-In-View. Figure, Background, and Closure would have to be key syntactical ideas, since they continually occur. Another would be Edmund Husserl's Horizon—the vague container in which foreground and background occur—and "unutterable" would have to be included among the words that are uttered, so there would have to be a rule to avoid its contradictory use. There would have to be a way to say we are Bracketing Off—*paying* attention to part of the whole field. I don't know if such a positivistic language of actual experiencing is constructible,[2] but its strangeness is a sure sign that people don't think they do experience in this way, whether or not they do. Some poets, however—Rilke, Mallarmé, Wordsworth—sometimes mold their sentences in this direction.

Common speech has a mixed parentage. It is empirical and formal, mental and behaviorist, physical and sociological, actual and abstract, and add plenty of historical accidents. Its names are often bastards and the syntax is therefore vague and inconsistent. But therefore it has leeway and potentiality for saying new things. Its inchoateness

2. German speculative philology has always gone in for this kind of interpretation of *natural* languages. E.g. at present, Eugene Rosenstock-Huessy tells us that there are four possible kinds of sentence: Fiativum, Subjectivum, Perfectum, and Abstractum ("he loves," "he courts," "he marries," "he has a wife"), which he obviously has drawn from the process of contacting the environment; and these are the proper moods of sentences for Drama, Lyrical Poetry, Epic, and Scientific Analysis—in the vein of Vico, Goethe-Schiller, and Victor Hugo.

Rosenstock-Huessy reproaches modern man for neglecting the first three "living" moods for the dead Abstractum, or indicative. To my mind, "he has a wife" is not abstract but habitual, which is often the most poignantly actual mood. Later in this chapter, we shall see that Chomsky derives the first three moods as transforms of the fourth.

is its efficiency. A danger of any definite constructed language, developed abstractly, is that it will impose on and prejudge experience and decide *a priori* what can be said.

To prejudge would be disastrous, especially for a language of science, which is hypothetical and probabilistic and thrives on freedom of inquiry; and in his *Logical Syntax* Carnap worries this problem a good deal. He comes to the formula that in their separate fields of work empirical scientists can use their ordinary language, but

> translatability into the formal mode of speech constitutes the touchstone for . . . all sentences which do not belong to the language of any one of the empirical sciences.

These must be sayable as sentences of grammar or logic, or they are incapable of rational discussion—that is, the language of *Logical Syntax* is a glue connecting the languages of empirical sciences, so as to exclude metaphysics and other delusions.

But has it been the case in the history of thought that "empirical science" is itself a definite notion? More particularly, is the distinction between object names and grammar always sharp in the on-going process of inquiry? Can "philosophical" questions really be kept from intruding? Consider a couple of examples:

In a well-known experiment of Gestalt psychology, a chicken pecks, not at a particular shade of gray, but at whichever is the darker of two shades; it responds to the relation rather than the atomic patches of color. Now suppose that it were the general pattern of behavior of animals to respond to such relations rather than to related qualities, then it would be a more vernacular scientific language to introduce a relation, e.g. "being darker," as a property of the name of the Gestalt, of one thing rather than two or more things, disobeying Russell's rule that we mentioned above, that relations connect two or more things. And the atomic elements, e.g. the different shades of gray, would have to be coped with in some other way. This would be a refinement in grammar of some importance. And I suggest that it would accompany a marked shift in scientific outlook.

Again, our usual notion of space is a room containing places named by Cartesian coordinates. But there is a long tradition that regards space rather as a kind of function of objects—the relation among the places of objects, e.g. in Aristotle, in the seventeenth century Vorticists, and somewhat in Einstein. Now suppose that new data and theory found this to be an increasingly necessary way of explanation; then it would certainly become vernacular to name places otherwise than by Cartesian coordinates, and every book of physics would look very different.

Something quite like this did occur with the passing of the phlogiston theory in chemistry. All formulas for chemical reactions came to be written differently; some previous elements became compounds, some previous compounds became elements, and phlogiston ceased to be written in.

During the past generation, introspective sentences have similarly dropped out of books and textbooks of "Psychology" (which has become, instead, "Behavioral Science.") In effect, such sentences are treated as ungrammatical; it is not proper to *say* them.

In principle, it should be easy simply to translate from one scientific language to the other, and so keep the grammar vernacular, elegantly following actual scientific thinking and operation. But historically, in cases of *grammatical* change, there is always a severe wrench of attitude; the grammar turns out to be not a convention but a world view. When scientists use a different grammar, it means they are looking in different directions and will come up with new experiments, data, and theory; the old attitude and language are not translated but outmoded, sometimes unwisely disregarded.

Conversely, an obligatory tight grammar does impose on experience. Those who talk the right etiquette are listened to, others are not. As C. D. Broad put it, "The editor of *Nature* seems to think that he is the Author of nature." This is not the intention of positivist empiricism, but there it is. "In the highly developed Indo-European languages," says Malinowski, "a sharp distinction can be drawn between the grammatic and lexical functions of words"—yes, except precisely in the critical cases where new conceptions and new attitudes are emerging, and we again all become primitives.

So, against Carnap, I do not think there can be a rule for the appropriate use of formal or vernacular language. Formal language can be prophylactic, but it can then become either pedantic and irrelevant, or it may prejudge experience and impose on it. The best is to try for a vernacular that molds itself to what is going on and to use it critically.

What is "matter-of-fact," what is "concrete," is often not so plain as positivist linguists seem to think. There may be social preconceptions concealed. Consider a topic like the primary education of children. There are certain functions that, rightly or wrongly, most people in America think ought to be performed: baby-sitting the children and relieving the home, children being company for one another, children learning to read and write, maybe learning democratic ways. These could be addressed as concrete problems, to be solved perhaps singly, perhaps together. Instead, people always speak of "schools," and these become the particulars for discussion and reform; but as soon as we bring in schools, there are entirely different problems, like relevant curriculum, motivating the children, skyrocketing costs, teacher training. Yet all these school problems might be quite unnecessary for performing the desired functions. But it is quite impossible to get people to talk about education without meaning schools. Can this "misplaced concreteness" be solved by a rule? Since people take the institution of schools *as* the nature of things, it would require a revolutionary cultural change for them to speak otherwise.

2 . Basic Vocabulary

Basic English, a less drastic reconstruction of common language, was designed primarily to be an auxiliary international language, but it was also to be a prophylaxis. C. K. Ogden said,

> Basic at last gives us a chance of getting free from the strange power which words have had over us from the earliest times; a chance of getting clear about the processes by which our ideas become fixed forms of behavior.

> Through Basic even the very young may be trained to a sense of true values.

The strategy is to select the smallest matter-of-fact vocabulary and simplest constructions of natural language, in terms of which everything desired can be said. This allows for more control of one's meaning and the policing of errors. In their intimate and work groups, we saw, people do drastically restrict their vocabulary and grammar, though they know many more words and constructions. It is the assumption of Basic that there is a common denominator of such restricted language that can serve for public communication and help everybody to mean the same thing by their sentences; and by being bound to the pragmatism of common everyday experience, it can help to diminish meaningless and superstitious sentences.

Tourist manuals, of course, have always tried to give the most useful common words for the most frequent occasions.[3] Historically, because of trade, diplomacy, travel, and military occupation, certain languages become *lingua franca*. And in the wake of the American empire in the wake of the British Empire, English is now the chief *lingua franca,* so that Ogden's idea of an international Basic English is plausible. Besides, except for its unfortunate spelling, English has peculiar virtues for the purpose: It is not much inflected, and it has the remarkable faculty of using the same word as noun, adjective, or verb, depending on the word order, which cuts down the necessary vocabulary.

Nevertheless, Basic English is not a live option. A generation ago it was solidly supported by Franklin Roosevelt and Winston Churchill, to the extent of doing nothing about it. Nowadays it would be considered imperialistic to press it, and 700 million Chinese would never buy it.

But it is instructive to consider if any such Basic language, carefully thought out, is valuable for native speakers, to de-mystify speech and clarify thought. I doubt it.

I agree that there are familiar matter-of-fact things, acts, relations, and feelings that all people experience and whose names could comprise the reservoir for a Basic vocabulary. (Note that there is here no prejudice for names

3. It is curious that tourist manuals have not been bolder. Since their aim is communication, they might include less regular speech and suggest methods of non-verbal communication: how to form an understandable pidgin, how to make native gestures, and how to interpret tones and facial expressions that are different from ours. Frankly, I have usually found them quite useless for *my* particular purposes; and I suppose that each person's most important purposes are not common purposes.

of physical objects or numbers, as in positivist languages. Basic includes "town," "family," "pain," "happy," "want," "hate.") These can be statistically determined. Next, Ogden excludes many words of everyday use and simple science, like "candle" or "latitude," which can be shortly well enough explained by other words. Next, following his prophylactic bent, he excludes thousands of unnecessary abstractions—what he calls "fiction"—which can be put more directly, e.g. saying "being free" instead of "liberty." And finally, he does not like names that are "unnecessarily colored by feeling" (I am not sure what this means).

In the vocabulary of Basic English, it works out as follows (I italicize words that are in Basic): There is *"town,"* but not "city" or "village." There is *"music"* and *"art,"* but not "poem." There are no words for "pride" or "envy," but "wrath," "sloth," "gluttony," "avarice," and "lechery" could be explained by *"angry," "lazy," "food," "money,"* and *"sex."* Basic allows *"law," "authority," "rule," "committee," "flag,"* but not "just," "prudent," "temperate," or "brave." There are *"mind," "thought,"* and *"ill,"* but not "insane" or "crazy"—my guess is that Ogden would explain these as "mental illness." There is *"regret"* and *"pain,"* but not "sad" or "sorrow." There is *"science,"* but not "morals," "ethics," "politics," or "beauty."

Obviously one could comment endlessly on one man's or a committee's list of basic ideas. I myself would find it impossible, for instance, to define a "village" or a "poem" in brief words, and I would make them basic. To give a neat brief definition of "pride" or "envy" requires the acumen of Spinoza in "On Human Bondage." Some would say that "mind" and "law" are rather fictional and best introduced more realistically. But any such *a priori* list of what is sayable necessarily imposes a point of view, and even a metaphysical theory, on the speakers. It is astonishing that Ogden does not seem to appreciate this.

The crucial error of the Basic approach, it seems to me, is that everybody has many plain words, which he uses confidently and with some clarity in his intimate speech and on important occasions, but which do not come from the same ambience as the matter-of-fact public speech of the Basic words and which therefore cannot be explained by them, for instance, "envy," "jealous," "pride," "poem," "justice," "trust." Such words are not un-empirical: they are learned in definite concrete situations, often the most important situations, but their designates cannot be pointed at. Ogden says,

> The natural development is from simple pointing, at the level of sign-language, to the more complex needs of normal talk.

Human language is not like that. The effect of trying to explain ideas which are plain and experiential to oneself in matter-of-fact public language is not to "get free from the strange power of words" nor to "train to a sense of true values"; rather, it is to stupefy; it is the baffled frustration of trying to talk politics or philosophy in a foreign language of which one knows only a tourist manual.

Traditional pedagogy makes more sense: We refine and correct our meanings not by limiting vocabulary but by using more and different words with finer nuances. It is better for everybody to have a bigger active vocabulary and to learn to use it appropriately, if need be stubbornly, but also honestly, asking: Do I really need this fancy word? Again, there is no linguistic rule, only moral virtue and literary judgment.

Genetically, the "natural development" is not from sign language to normal speech, nor are the basic public words elementary. If it were true that, in picking up language, there were a development from the simpler to the more complex—with corresponding corruption by confusion and mistakes—then it would make sense to go back to simpler and more innocent elements and reconstruct. But primitive speech is usually more syntactically complicated than civilized speech. Folk speech is often as corrupt as fancy speech learned in a more urbane context. Children's speech is not essentially simpler than adult speech. A small child does not speak monosyllables and then polysyllables; he can lisp "Tyrannosaurus Rex" as readily as he can say "cow"—in New York or London a middle class child is more likely to know the former object than the latter, at least its bones. My children at six sometimes said "consume" instead of "eat" and "reply" instead of "answer." Some two-year-olds make correct complex sentences. We saw that Chomsky is so taken by the ability of two-year-olds to abstract grammatical forms from the speeches that they hear that he says this algebra is as if innate. Despite the current notion, after Piaget and Vygotsky, that logical and scientific reasoning develops pretty late, an eleven-month-old can make a practical disjunctive syllogism: e.g. I appear in the room and she makes a bee-line for the typewriter in the other room, as if saying, "Ah, since he's here, he's not there to push me away." If I remember, this is the last syllogism in Aristotle's *Prior Analytics.*

As a means of literature, a Basic vocabulary can be valuable. As speech, it may be frustrating and insensitive, but as deliberate writing, it is fresh and plain. I think I recall a Basic translation of Homer, in which "quiver" was rendered as "box of arrows" rather than "box of pointed sticks used to shoot with"; but it would certainly be awkward to translate the *Iliad* without "arrows." Yet, if persisted in, a Basic vocabulary can provide a lively shock of matter-of-factness. Suppose we spell out "quiver" into a full Homeric simile: ". . . box full of pointed sticks that had feathers from the hawk that used to dive from the sky onto a Thracian field and stun the hare . . . steered through the air by these feathers acting like a rudder, the point of the stick pierced Ajax, etc." Just as with the languages of Russell and Carnap, a program of language reform might not work as prophylaxis, yet might turn up a good style for poetry.

In candor, I must conclude these remarks on prophylactic languages with a confession that may fatally discredit me. Language reforms like those of Ogden and Richards or Carnap tend to treat equally excellent intellects of the past as if they were little better than idiots who were caught in verbal traps, not wrestling with living experience. My own reading of the problems of philosophy has been that philosophers of the past were not abused by language. They used the language and conceptions of their times and twisted them to say their own say; when I think away their old-fashioned formulations, as I usually can, I have almost always found that there remains a puzzling problem to wrestle with, that they did wrestle with and suggest a solution to restate in our own terms. I have not been impressed by any vast number of pseudo-problems that have been liquidated by merely linguistic analysis. Some have just been swept under the rug; others are replaced by problems created by the new method—e.g. "How can a conventional language be applied?"—others reappear in other contexts—they become "psychological" or "emotive," which doesn't help if emotions have cognitive content, which they do. In my opinion, the history of philosophy is better told by the magnificent tribute that T. H. Green paid to Kant: "When the nature of things is clear, Kant is easy; when Kant is difficult, we find that the nature of things is puzzling."

Many problems of philosophy and ways of talking about them are no longer with us; this is rarely because they have been explained away, but because, like other good and bad causes of history, they are not interesting in changed circumstances. People do not care about them any more; on the wheel of change they may come to care about them again.

In my own case, I have never, except for momentary colloquial convenience, used the words "concept," "idea," "mind," "thinking," "will," or even "purpose"—despite the fact that I consider myself a Kantian and am an author in psychology. I have not given much attention to the actions that these words try to name. But it is because in psychotherapy, either as patient or therapist, I concentrated on behavior; as a writer and literary critic, I concentrated on poems and their structures; and I grew up breathing the air of Jamesian pragmatism, which has seemed to me to be politically right and, if I may say so, in the American grain. Yet European phenomenologists, for whom I feel a strong affinity (for instance, in *Gestalt Therapy* and in this present book) continually use a mentalist language. It must be useful to them, since I like what they come out with; but I reformulate it.

3 . Simplest Grammar

The method of constructing a positivist grammar is to find or postulate the fewest possible grammatical forms and spin out from them, by rule, the forms of the rest of the sentences. As with the Basic vocabulary, this was not, of course, the historical development of the language; nor is it how children learn to speak. Chomsky, the best known of the structuralist grammarians, specifically advises against using such a method in pedagogy, rather than letting the child do his own grammar-forming. But the structural model would be capital for making programs for translation- and other language-machines—e.g. Chomsky's *Syntactic Structures* was paid for by technological corporations. My own humanistic caution about the method is, again, that this is not how grammar *is;* it does not show its vital impulse which is, as with the rest of language, to say what needs to be said.

Chomsky says,

> When we actually try to set up for English the simplest grammar, we find that the kernel consists of simple declarative active sentences . . . and that all other sentences can be described more simply as transformations of these.

As I have already suggested, this proposition does not do justice to the imperatives (which Bloomfield called the *other* "favorite sentence-form" in English). In the second person, imperatives do not have subjects; to derive them from declaratives, it is necessary to understand a "you" in ellipses as the subject, but this is an artifact.

The vocatives, "Mary!" "Hey you!" are a summons to be a hearer to a speaker; they are not yet subjects of sentences. When, by exception, an imperative has "you," it is uttered as a vocative—"You! Watch out!"—it is not a subject. When the utterance is, "You watch out," it means "You'd better watch out"—not an imperative.

Historically, second person imperative forms are always aboriginal and have short and sometimes clipped forms of the root. And an unusual proportion of imperatives have exclamation points. My claim is that Chomsky's derivation is too simple and misses the actual use and depoverishes it: The essence of imperatives is direct action, not declaration about.

In the first person, we say the imperative periphrastically, "Let's go!" To understand a "you" here would be

most peculiar. And when the third person does have a
subject, as in "Long live the king!" "Hallowed be Thy
name," "God damn it!" the form seems to be derived otherwise, indirectly from some kind of subjunctive or optative.

Turn now to sentences in the passive construction. Are
they all transforms of active sentences? Again I think not.
But my intuition is that the situation is here the opposite
of the imperatives. Imperatives were always words of direct
action, but English never did have a conjugation to say
the passive in a simple way. According to Sweet, the only
true passive form in Anglo-Saxon is *hātte,* "he hight,"
surviving from an older stage. Thus, to express passive
meaning, speakers periphrastically inverted and transformed active sentences, and this is exactly how Chomsky
derives passive sentences. Nevertheless, *there has been a
continuing effort to say true passives, whether or not an
active agent is part of the experience.* Speakers have tried
to say the experience of something happening not in their
control, of being carried along, of being "thrown" in the
situation, as Heidegger puts it. Therefore, there spring up
anomalous passive sentences that are heard as perfectly
grammatical but that cannot be derived, except factitiously,
from active kernels.

To derive passives, Chomsky postulates three main
rules: Passives can be derived only from transitive verbs;
the passive must not be followed directly by a noun phrase,
which would be like a direct object; a verb followed by
"by + Noun" must be in the passive. These rules will take
us from "John ate lunch" to "lunch was eaten by John."
But let's try them on other passives.

Consider first expressions like "he was hurt in the accident," "he is hated in the village," "the wound was
healed," "she was blessed with children," "I'm damned if
I will." What are the agents here? It is factitious to say that
there is an active agent in the offing: "hurt (by the car),"

"hated (by everybody)," "blessed (by God)"—the speaker does not mean that. It is possible to assert, of course, that the verbs have become adjectives, but I don't believe it. We would then have to claim that "he was hurt by the truck" is too dissimilar from "he was hurt in the accident." And more tellingly, what would we do with the now acceptable "he got hurt," where "hurt" is rather clearly a verb, as in "he got carried along by the current"? [4] Further, in at least one of these cases, I am not satisfied that the verb is transitive: "My finger was healed" is like "my finger healed," which I will soon suggest is a Middle voice trying to express itself as in Greek. I would derive the passive in such a case from the intransitive Middle verb.

(It is clear from these examples that I do not at all disagree with Chomsky's fine insight that speakers transform sentences and make up the language; we are indebted to him for his careful demonstration of it. It is only his English grammar that is poor and his reductionism that does not work.)

In a form developed quite recently, the progressive passive, e.g. "the house is being built," it would be awkward, if not impossible, to say that the verb is an adjective. (The construction replaces the sequence "the house is on building," "the house is a-building," "the house is building," but the last of these is apparently *too* anomalous, although I myself like it and sometimes use it. But we have all agreed to accept "What's doing?") It is precisely on this new use that A. C. Baugh comments:

This history of the new progressive passive shows that English is a living and growing thing. . . . If the need

4. When there is a different form for adjective and participle, we begin to border on the ambiguous as to what is adjective and what is verb: "The door was open (*adj.*), but I don't know when it was opened (*verb without agent*)." "The door was closed (*adj.? verb?*), but I don't know when it was closed (*verb*)."

is felt for a new and better way of expressing an idea, we may rest assured that a way will be found.

Yes.

Proceed now to an indefinitely long series of sentences like "I'm surprised you came so early," "She was baffled, astonished, etc., that he believed it," "I'm impressed that you understand it." It would be a high price to pay for a rule to call all these adjectives. If they are verbs, they are followed by noun clauses and do not comply with Chomsky's rule that the passive must not be followed directly by a noun phrase. In any interpretation, however, it is puzzling (to me) how to parse the noun clauses. The construction seems to be anomalous.

By inversion, it is easy to get dubious active sentences from these passive sentences: "That you came so early surprised me"; "That he believed it astonished her." Nevertheless, these dubious subjects cannot be used with "by" to express the active agent in the passive construction. It is necessary to introduce an entirely factitious ellipsis: "She was surprised (by the fact) that he came so early." Indeed, *these cases do not have the same meaning as regularly transformed active sentences.* If we compare "She was astonished at his arrival" or "that he arrived" with "She was astonished by his arrival," the first set means that her expectation of things was jarred; the second may mean the same, but it may also mean that his arrival, perhaps at the door, upset *her,* not her expectation; it is a true agent. In "I'm surprised that you came so early," the noun clause is the content of my surprise; it is what I am surprised at. But in "I'm surprised by your early arrival," the noun might be, in one interpretation, the cause of my surprise, an agent.

It is because of a simplistic analysis that the dictionary (Random House) lists certain past participles as adjectives,

e.g. "resolved," "determined." Consider the series "I resolved the question," "I resolved to do it," "I am resolved
to do it"; "I determined the boundary," "I determined to
do it," "I am determined to do it." I would suggest that
"I resolved to do it" and "I determined to do it" are *not*
transitive verbs with "to do" as the direct object; rather,
they are intransitive verbs with a middle sense: The action
remains with and on the subject himself. This middle
meaning, "I resolved myself," like "I made up my mind,"
clearly cannot have a proper direct object, and so "to do
it" is a syntactical anomaly. (In "I made up my mind to do
it," "to do it" is probably "in apposition.") In turn, "I
am resolved" and "I am determined" are not adjectives but
passives, the internal action having gone a step further, so
that the subject is now fixed—he has *been* resolved and
determined.

I seem to be rather lightly using the notion of anomaly,
but one simply cannot regard "to do it" as a direct object
in the sense that "resolved the question," "determined the
boundary," have direct objects. And the struggle of speakers to find an authentic passive construction—and an authentic Middle construction (I shall return to this)—has
led to other anomalies. Consider, "he was given a book,"
where the *indirect* object of the active sentence has become
the subject, and "book" is called the retained object!—
Object of what?—On the other hand, in "he was named
John," we seem to have a retained apposition.—In what
case is "John," nominative or objective?

In this context, let me return to Chomsky's remark
which I quoted in the preceding chapter,

> Grammar is best formulated as a self-contained study
> independent of semantics. . . . The notion of "struc-
> tural meaning" appears to be quite suspect. It is ques-
> tionable that the grammatical devices available in

language are used consistently enough so that meaning can be assigned to them directly.

I disagreed with this, arguing that the meanings of grammatical forms were usually consistent enough (e.g. forms for tenses), and that just because they were broad and sometimes vague they could serve their function in speech, to give the hearer the *drift* of what was being said, which he could fill in with the lexical words. If the grammar said nothing substantive, communication would be incredibly difficult and slow.[5]

5. But the chief use of a constructed simplest grammar is, I surmise, to program language-machines, which don't need to catch the drift and which can whirr on fast. I am not competent to discuss this, but let me quote a generally relevant passage from *New Reformation,* pp. 16–17:

A question of immense importance for the immediate future is, Which functions should be automated or organized to use business machines, and which should not? This question is not getting asked, and the present disposition is that the sky is the limit for extraction, refining, manufacturing, processing, packaging, ticketing, transactions, information retrieval, recruitment, middle management, evaluation, diagnosis, instruction, and even research and invention. [I should have added translation and the determination of grammatical sentences.] Whether the machines can do all these kinds of jobs and more is partly an empirical question, but it also partly depends on what is meant by doing a job. Very often, for example in college admissions, machines are acquired for putative economies (which do not eventuate), but the true reason is that an overgrown and over-centralized organization cannot be administered without them. The technology conceals the essential trouble, perhaps that there is no community of the faculty and that students are treated like things. The function is badly performed and finally the system breaks down anyway. I doubt that enterprises in which interpersonal relations are very important are suited to much programming.

But worse, what can happen is that the real function of an enterprise is subtly altered to make it suitable for the mechanical system. (For example, "information retrieval" is taken as an adequate replacement for critical scholarship.) Incommensurable factors, individual differences, local context, the weighting of evi-

Now I go further. The transformations that speakers make, deriving new sentence forms, must be interpreted in two directions: Like all behavior, speaking operates creatively not only *from what the speaker has* (the inherited code) but *toward the end-in-view* (what needs to be said in the situation). And the hearer creatively adjusts to what is going on. Thus, I have defined language as the tension between the inherited code and what needs to be said, and between the speaker and the hearer. In these tensions there arise anomalies. When an anomaly is broadly relevant to the situation, is "logical," it will be heard as grammatical; and if the situation is typical, it will become grammatical. Jespersen puts it well. It is the genius of English, he says, that

> where the logic of facts or of the exterior world is at war with the logic of grammar, English is free from the narrow-minded pedantry which in most languages sacrifices the former to the latter or makes people shy of saying or writing things which are not "strictly grammatical."

---

dence, are quietly overlooked, though they may be of the essence. The system, with its subtly transformed purposes, seems to run very smoothly, it is productive, and it is more and more out of line with the nature of things and the real problems. Meantime the system is geared in with other enterprises of society, and its products are taken at face value. Thus, major public policy may depend on welfare or unemployment statistics which, as they are tabulated, are not about anything real. In such a case, the particular system may not break down; the whole society may explode.

I need hardly point out that American society is peculiarly liable to the corruption of inauthenticity. Busily producing phony products, it lives by public relations, abstract ideals, front politics, show-business communications, mandarin credentials. It is preeminently overtechnologized. And computer technologists especially suffer the euphoria of being in a new and rapidly expanding field. It is so astonishing that a robot can do the job at all, or seem to do it, that it is easy to blink at the fact that he is doing it badly or isn't really doing quite the job.

4 . Literary Grammar

For the purposes of literature, our aim would be the opposite of making a Basic vocabulary or constructing a simplest grammar. It would be to explore the anomalies, the little-used forms, the salvageable old-fashioned, and the genius of English in order to provide writers with the richest possible language. Historically, for instance, this occurred during the Renaissance: Latin words were introduced which were doubles of Norman words, but instead of the older words being driven out, some survived with different meanings—"royal," "regal"; "loyal," "legal"—preserving the older feudalism in the new Statism. With the simplification of the Anglo-Saxon declensions, sometimes different cases survived with different meanings: "shade," "shadow." At present I am trying to maintain the English spelling "subtile" to mean fine, discriminating, along with the American spelling "subtle" to mean cunningly clever; but editors and proofreaders undo me. Some of us—let me mention Dwight MacDonald as an ally—have been fighting a losing fight to save "disinterested," which the young take to mean uninterested; but the word is irreplaceable; it does not mean impartial (I give my friend disinterested advice, but not impartial advice).

On the other hand, there are artificial distinctions that add nothing and are usefully disregarded, like the symmetrical rule "I shall, you will. I will! you shall!" These usually have no historical warrant but are invented by grammarians. History is full of outmoded relics, but it always has style.

Pursuing the discussion of active and passive a step further, let me say something about the Middle voice in English. English is a wonderfully various and plastic language, but one of its defects, contrasted with Greek for example, is that it has no explicit Middle voice to say an important way of being in the world. The Middle voice of a verb says that the subject is simply present and concerned in the environment, engaged, perhaps moving, perhaps motionless, but not acting on anything or being acted on. I am especially interested in this modality because it is like a desirable attitude in psychotherapy, non-attachment, which is hard to explain to English-speaking patients. Disinterestedness is a non-attached attitude.[6]

The Middle voice is badly explained as reflexive, e.g. by Goodwin:

> In the [Greek] middle voice the subject is represented as acting on himself or in some manner which concerns himself.

But acting on the self is far too active and voluntaristic, and far too passive and masochistic, to express simple presence or moving-in-and-with-the-environment. But some languages, like French, do use reflexive forms to say Middle meanings, e.g. *"il s'amuse,"* "he has a good time." Here there is no nuance of acting on himself; rather, he is there in a certain way. We similarly say, "he enjoys himself," in English, but the usage is rare, whereas in French it is a regular expedient.

But in English, the so-called intransitive verbs often have a Middle meaning. It may sometimes depend on the interpretation. If we take "to walk" as meaning to traverse

6. Jespersen is uncharacteristically insensitive on this topic. His single comment (in *The Philosophy of Grammar*) is: "On the middle voice, as found for instance in Greek, there is no necessity to say much here, as it has no separate notional character of its own. Sometimes it is purely reflexive, sometimes it denotes a vaguer reference to the subject, sometimes it is purely passive, and sometimes scarcely to be distinguished from the ordinary active. In some verbs it has developed special semantic values not easily classified." It would be strange if a major form were quite this pointless! especially to Jespersen who believed strongly that form had meaning.

the environment, it is an active verb; if we take it as the self-initiated behavior of locomotive animals, it is Middle. The French distinguish these two as *"marcher"* and *"se promener."* So we can doubly interpret many of the elementary intransitives: "go," "come," "stay," "stand," "sit," "rise," "sleep." It is likely that it is this ambiguity, between active and Middle meanings, that causes the indecision as to whether such intransitives are to be conjugated with "have" or "be." Anglo-Saxon conjugates them with "be," providing a form for the meaning. French conjugates some simply with "be" (*"il est allé,"* *"il est venu"*) and some as reflexives with "be" (*"il s'en est allé,"* *"il s'est endormi"*). Modern English has generally opted for "have," but there are survivals of the older form ("begone," "he is come," "He is risen"). In colloquial speech ("he's gone," "he's come back"), it is hard to tell which auxiliary is being used.

The Middle meaning of intransitives becomes much more clear-cut when a verb is both transitive and intransitive, and the intransitive has a different lexical meaning: "he bathes the dog," "he bathes" (Fr. *"il se bagne,"* Gr. λούεται). So: "he breathes the air," "he breathes"; "he moves the chair," "he moves to Boston"; "it reflects the light," "he reflects on it"; "he speaks the language," "he speaks for the motion"; "he figured the sum," "it figures"; "he feels the texture," "he feels well"; "he hurt his finger," "his finger hurts"; "he mends the dish," "his finger is mending"; "he forms it," "it forms"; "he transforms it to," "it transforms into"; "he used the fork," "he used to go"; "he rolls the ball," "he rolls downhill"; "he turns the wheel," "he turns away"; "David fights Goliath," "they fight." In many such cases, the English intransitive is a French reflexive: *"il se tourne,"* *"ils se battent."* And rather rarely, English goes the same route: "he helped me out," "he helped himself to the cake"; "he enjoyed it," "he enjoyed himself."

Then, as a further complication, English has a genius to

make anything into a verb, and the Middle-meaning intransitives become: "he walks the dog," "he stands it up,"
"he rests it on the table," "he stays its course," to mean "he
makes it stand," "he makes it rest," etc. The grammatical
effect is, of course, quite anomalous. The action in "he
stands it up" is divided between a certain activity on the
part of "he" and a Middle behavior of "it" with, now, a
nuance of passivity! This might seem to be a ridiculously
complex way of putting it, and yet it is what is actually
said.

"I determined the boundary," "I determined to go";
"he demonstrated the proposition," "we demonstrated in
front of the U.N.": Here the reflexive action of the Middle
verb is evident, turning the action on the self—and we saw
that this may transform into a true passive: "I was determined to go"; "I was resolved to do it." Sometimes, however, there seems to be both a simple Middle and a reflexive Middle: "he works the machine," "the clock works,"
"he works at home" (= "he works himself at home"?).

It is clear from these cases which I have collected at
random that the basic grammatical category is not intran-
sitivity but Middle voice—I do not see the point of the
designation "v.i." ("verb intransitive") so meticulously used
by the dictionaries. The verbs do not take direct objects,
because their action stops with the subjects or is sometimes
turned *on* the subjects, leading to transformations into true
passives. The heavy emphasis on the distinction between
transitive and intransitive verbs is an artifact of grammarians.

The three languages I have had in mind use three different grammatical expedients: In Greek, the Middle forms
rather closely resemble the passives; in French, they are
active verbs with reflexive objects, conjugated with *être*;
in English, the verb has no object—its action does not pass
on. All these are plausible ways in which speakers use

available forms in the language to say what importantly needs saying.

Also, nuances of voice are expressed by the plastic variation of prepositions, e.g. "he was surprised by her arrival," "he was surprised at her arrival"; "he transforms it to," "it transforms into." In German such prepositions can be incorporated as prefixes into the verbs, with a change of meaning in the dictionary.

Let me return a moment to my special interest in the Middle voice in psychotherapy. Consider the current dispute about the "Calvinist Ethic." The Calvinist says, "Do a job," with an active meaning; the Hippie says, "Do your thing," with a Middle meaning. The issue is not between Doing and Being, as it is usually expressed, for there is very little Being or "just living" without doing something in the environment. But the issue is what is the grammatical voice of the doing. Nobody would deny that English has overused the active voice, and we ought to strengthen the Middle voice. As it is, everybody—both Calvinists and Hippies—find themselves thrown into the passive, though that too is sometimes a good way of being in the world.

This kind of speculation is not very useful for traditional grammars that are concerned with the correct application of the common code; and speakers do mold their sentences according to the code, whatever it happens to be. But it is useful for understanding and enriching the code, and speakers do modify the code to say their say.

There is no rule for right linguistic method.

—I keep repeating the formula "There is no rule for (the topic under discussion)." It is in the nature of the case. It is in the nature of language. Speech is bound to an inherited social code, to the empirical world it has to talk about, and perhaps to epistemological imperatives. But speaking is spontaneous and it is artistic, and like all behavior it has an end-in-view. Somehow good spoken sentences must resolve these contraries.

My bias as a man of letters is that it is best to do linguistics like natural history or art criticism, reasoned but *a posteriori,* rather than like mathematics, as is the current style. Present-day linguists and nineteenth century philologists have made too much of a big deal of prediction, predicting the forms that will occur. It is soul-satisfying to have one's prediction confirmed, but it is not terribly important except in sciences that are applied, as physics to engineering, and where the consequences must be controlled. The chief use of humanistic studies is to explain, to understand, to appreciate. And in linguistics we want to make sense precisely of novelty, unique appropriateness, history, and even accident—they are *expected* factors.

Let me make a close analogy. In literary criticism it is possible to define literary genres and predict from them. But in analysis it will be found that only hack works conform to the genres. Powerful works are *sui generis;* they sometimes set themselves absurd conditions and carry it off—consider a really crazy work like Handel's *Messiah.* This does not mean that powerful works are incomprehensible; on the contrary, most (not all) excellent works are rather transparently demonstrated. But we cannot know one before it has been invented. Similarly, it is possible to take a statistical average of speech events and abstract a structure from it that has routine application. But this deceptively makes us think we understand something when we don't; examples of excellent speech may not fall in the average—and I have been arguing that they are *likely not to.* The most intimate speech, the most convivial speech, the most expressive speech, the most poetic speech are likely to be "deviant." But they are not deviant; they can be reasoned *a posteriori.*

Thus, I think that Roman Jakobson's testy remark is wrong-headed, that "idiolect is a perverse fiction . . . everything in language is socialized." The issue is not whether speakers have a private language—of course they do not—but whether good socialization (and good society) does not require spontaneity, concreteness, and invention in the intercourse of its members.

CHAPTER VIII

Complex-Words and Poetry

1 . Aboriginal Language

In pursuit of a grammar for literature, let us now look in a very different direction, to the ingenious reconstruction by Jespersen of the language of Adam and Eve. (The present-day ridicule of this subject is pretty disgusting and philistine. If human beings do not speculate about the origin of language, about what should they speculate?) I shall try to show that, better than he knew, Jespersen sketched out the structure of the language of sophisticated poetry.

Before Jespersen, the usual method for reconstructing the prehistoric language was, so to speak, geographical. By abstracting the elements that the scattered languages had in common, scholars concluded what must have been the stock from which they diffused. This method is inevitably reductive, and the language consisted of simple roots appropriate to the grunts of simple cavemen. Jespersen's method is historical, and he comes out with the opposite result—extreme complexity. He studies the changes in various languages that we know over historical periods, and if there seems to have been a strongly continuous evolution in one direction—except for occasional perturbations —he feels justified in extrapolating backward to the unknown period from which the evolution started. Aboriginal language differed from ancient language as ancient language differed from modern language, only more so. He then checks his results against languages of existing primitive peoples and the babbling of infants.

Besides, as is generally characteristic of his linguistics, if he can show language-forming tendencies in present speakers that are not yet codified in correct language, he is willing to attribute similar plastic power to aborigines. Thus, since he can show that we often invent imitative-echoic words and "they may be just as linguistically fertile as any other part of vocabulary," he allows our ancestors to have said "bow wow." And since we express and codify emotional interjections and natural signs of the rhythm and effort of physical labor, he allows them to say "pooh pooh" and "yo heave ho." Since small talk and the mush talk of lovers do not now make much sense, he assumes that they probably never did, and he takes us back to chattering monkeys and crooners. In my opinion, all this is grossly uncritical and right as rain, especially since Jespersen did not take himself too seriously, though he took the subject seriously.

The evolution of modern languages, Jespersen finds, has been by and large toward simplification and standardization. They have "short elements, freely and regularly combinable." Ancient languages, and *a fortiori* the aboriginal language, consisted of "inseparable irregular conglomerations." The basic words that have been resistant to change and have survived from antiquity are irregular in conjugation and declension: "be," "is," "was"; *"fero,"* *"tuli,"* *"latus";* *"aller,"* *"je vais,"* *"j'irai";* "good," "better"; *"bonus,"* *"melior,"* *"optimus";* "I," "me"; "one," "two," "three," "four," "five." Ancient word formation is intensely particularistic and anomalous: "cow," "bull," "heifer," "calf"; "horse," "mare," "stallion," "foal," "colt"; "nye of pheasants," "covey of quail," "bevy of cattle," "flock of sheep." Existing primitives carry this even further: "The Zulus have no word for 'cow' but words for 'red cow' 'black cow,' etc."; "in Cherokee, instead of one word for washing, we find different words according to what is washed, myself, my head, somebody else's head, my face, somebody else's face, clothes, dishes, a child." Whorf reasoned that such particularity may have metaphysical meaning: e.g. the Hopi can say "my floor," "my post," "my ceiling," but not "my room," since an empty space is nothing. Perhaps general terms are equivalent to empty space and are nothing?

Along with this, in ancient languages, goes a proliferation of specifically inflected tenses, moods, cases, and genders—causatives, optatives, frequentatives, historical presents, dual numbers, ablatives, instrumentals, locatives, intimate and public pronouns, high-birth and low-birth genders, animate and inanimate genders, etc., etc. More and more information is given in each inseparable word. Correspondingly, the word order of sentences can be extremely loose. (Jespersen is satisfied that all of this is true also for ancient Chinese, where it is usually denied.)

In principle, if we extrapolate backward this disposition to inflect everything, we should come to less and less distinction between grammatical and lexical meaning altogether.[1] When language is plastic, any apt formulation,

1. I do not mean that there is "in reality" no such distinction. All philosophic grammarians, whether Aristotle, Duns Scotus, Kant,

like "he goes-and-goes," "he sleeps-and-sleeps," can easily
become a grammatical tense, if it catches on and is repeated
as a form that can be filled in with other terms. It becomes
the Continuative Tense and will solemnly end up in the
Grammar. Viewed this way, there is no discrepancy between Jespersen's position that aboriginal language is
heavily grammatical and the findings of anthropologists
that at least some primitive tongues are quite skimpy in
tenses, moods, and cases.

The Trobriand language that Malinowski describes
presents an even deeper problem. It is weak in inflected
grammatical devices, yet it does *not* fill out the meaning, as
developed modern languages do, with lexical words. The
solution is that grammatical relations are given by playing
on routine formulas, by referring always to each concrete
situation, by how the speaker takes the situation, by his
tone and non-verbal behavior. Then it is hard to distinguish not only grammatical and lexical meaning, but
verbal and non-verbal meaning. In such a case, we could
say either that the "grammar" is bare or that it is im-
mensely complex, including the whole social etiquette.

The aboriginal language was more vividly metaphoric
than ancient languages, not to speak of modern languages.
The physical terms with which we express imperceptible
things or abstract concepts were then still alive and fresh,
whereas, says Jespersen, "the better stocked a language is

Carnap, or Chomsky, make grammar absolute, whether its grounding is metaphysical, epistemological, innate, or conventional. My
own view is that grammar is distinct from designations, and I
would ground it empirically in the phenomenology of being a
speaker or hearer. Since these spontaneously make speech, they
must shape it. Nevertheless, the distinction has to be gradually
critically delineated out of primitive confusion, just like all other
high philosophical distinctions; the grammar and the lexical meanings can never be stated once and for all, but must be distinguished
in every act of speech, at least in principle; and in inventive acts of
speech, which are frequent, we are back in the primitive confusion.

with ex-metaphors, the less need for going out of one's way to find new metaphors."

And early language was tonal and chant-like, just as in ancient forms of modern languages there is more use of tones to indicate lexical and syntactical differences. I would add that tonal inflection of phrases and sentences plays an immense part in intimate colloquial speech, that we would find it hard to parse, indicating not only question, statement, and command, but what is referred to, its relative importance, whether we approve or disapprove, respect or ridicule, whether it is urgent, whether we are resigned, and so forth. How much does a small child who does not have words to go by, or just a few words, nevertheless pick up by the tone? Some? A lot? Nearly all? Besides, aborigines were presumably more uninhibitedly passionate, and the speech of passion is more like crooning than ordinary speech is. Anyway, says Jespersen, simple folk and children sing more at their work and play.

Finally, modern languages are "analytic," with short words for units of meaning that they combine to form sentences. But with its elaborate inflections to express all kinds of relations and its concrete vocabulary that needed no modifiers, the aboriginal language consisted of long conglomerations that could say whole sentences in a word. Anthropologists have given us many beautiful examples of such conglomerations from primitive cultures. Buber cites a Fuegian word that means "they stare at one another, each waiting for the other to volunteer to do what both wish, but are not able to do." Louis Gray cites a Kwakiutl word, "that invisible man near me, I am told, lies ill on his back on the floor of the absent house away from you." Eskimo says in one word, "I am looking for something suitable for a fish line" (Bloomfield). Of these, the Fuegian word sounds—at least in translation—witty and poetic, the Kwakiutl pathetically clumsy, the Eskimo eminently practical, but all express a global involvement of the persons and the situation. Zulu for "far away" is "there where someone cries out 'O Mother, I am lost.'" Cree has a word for "that recently present but now out of sight," like Mallarmé's space from which the swan has just flown. In a story of mine, *Adam,* I try sophisticatedly to talk phenomenology in this language with conglomerations like "the man-moving-in-whichever-direction-brings-into-being-new-space."

2

When he comes to evaluate this remarkable reconstruction, however, Jespersen loses his inspiration. Instead of judging that such a language could be a plausible means of communication for a simple but highly communal and organic culture, he describes its speakers as being busy mainly with love calls and war songs and inventing denotation by calling outstanding personalities by proper names. This is not a wide discourse, and critics have seized on Jespersen's love calls to ridicule his theory of the origin of language, disregarding his ingenious method. For purposes of my own argument, let me defend it—in ways that Jespersen himself would strongly have disapproved.

In fact, Jespersen believed that ancient languages were inferior to modern ones. He believed that if a language could not say abstractions and general properties, it impeded thought; if word order was irregular, ideas were helter-skelter; if people expressed their emotions, they had no grasp of reality. He thought that the concrete particular is formless and cannot be said efficiently; that people have to have standardized means in order to cope economically with experience; that it is a great advantage to be able to make an indefinite number of combinations of small units.

Thus, he devoted hundreds of pages in his various books to arguing that modern languages have made steady progress in their evolution, toward rationalization, *away* from the aboriginal language which was not good for much.

But in my opinion, the issue should be stated as follows: There *are* advantages to standardizing, simplifying, and having elementary units of meaning—and anyway our culture does and must express itself by such means. But it is hard to get these advantages without sacrificing the immediacy, feelingfulness, and concrete reality that alone give speech its human meaning. These are not strong points of modern culture.

Jespersen's aboriginal language might not be so unworkable as he thought. Its deficiencies have compensating advantages. Take the particularism and irregularity of the vocabulary. The distinctions that people make depend on the actual work they are performing—a modern dairy farmer says "Jersey" and "Holstein" just as a Zulu might say "red cow" and "black cow." When people are closely engaged with their tasks, when their labor is not "alienated," every detail is worthy of attention and can have its proper name. Anthropological accounts of acculturation show that if a new function is taken on, requiring a new level of generalization, the language always manages to find a way to say it; but until then, it seems to me, the general term might be just loose talk and *in*efficient. For average folk there is no advantage in having indefinitely numerous combinations, since for their intimate speech they discard most of the words they know anyway.

Nor is it the case that using general or abstract terms is a superior use of the intellect. It depends on the kinds of problem one confronts. There are different kinds of reasoning. One can compare particulars and generalize and reason from the abstract classes, and this method has paid off handsomely in sciences where there are well-defined classes and the possibility of controlled experiment. Or one can find the structure *in* a concrete experience, perhaps a single one, and draw out consequences as properties of that whole, and this has been useful for natural history, medicine, and (in my opinion) the social sciences, where it is more important to understand unique cases than to discover general laws. Some people reason one way and some the other, and I guess the same might apply to whole cultures. (For some kinds of problem it is wiser not to reason too much by any method.) Long ago, Aristotle, who was not without intellect, complained that Plato's abstractions, hypothetical method, and method of class division were empty; in his opinion one could reason scientifically only from "real premises." [2] At present, we strongly favor the Pythagorean and Platonic style, but people who do not are not idiots.

Emotions do not necessarily hinder knowing. They may help it by brightening the figure against the background and by leading to relevant exploring. (John Dewey, too, was off on this point.) All emotions have a cognitive part; they say something about the environment in relation to the self: that it contains an obstacle, that it threatens physical safety or moral dignity, that it suits one's appetite, maybe that it has an empty spot and one will have to resign oneself to living without. The emotions are part of the motive power to cope; on Darwinian grounds, we would not have them if they had not proved useful for survival over a billion years. Normally, feeling, knowing, and action go together and reinforce one another, so that a language free to express and arouse feeling should indicate a people intelligent for their practical happiness,

2. If I remember, there is a similar statement by Darwin. After he had crashingly mis-explained the origin of coral islands, he swore that he would never again reason from "logic," from the excluded middle, but he would demand real evidence to start from.

whereas an affectless language should indicate a stupid culture. If history does not bear this out, one possible explanation is that historical conditions have rarely been normal.

In good cases, "irregular word order" is the order of the speaker's attention exploring the situation as it transpires for him. Jespersen claims that it makes difficulties for the listener; but if the listener is involved in the same situation and is in sympathy with the speaker, the speaker's word order might be the most efficient way of communicating. And a part of the speaker's order is the insertion of remarks directed *ad hoc* to the listener ("Do you follow me?" "No, pay attention to this, not to that."); this is exemplified in the Kwakiutl sentence about the sick man. Far from being helter-skelter, such ordering is psychologically economical, whereas a standardized order might require translation into and out of the standard, and interfere with spontaneous understanding.

The sesquipedalian words and the proliferation of inflections perform the function of keeping the whole speech event globally together, with its referents, moods, and persons; they diminish the danger of leaving out something important to either the facts or the feelings. I grant that a pedantic use of all those conjugations and declensions would be deadening; but why would preliterates be any more pedantic in their familiar speech than we are? The remains that we have from ancient India, Greece, and Rome are literary texts, and for literary purposes it is an advantage to spell out all the niceties, since just what is lacking is the transient feedback and steering of spoken language.

It is useful to place Jespersen historically. *Language* was published in 1922, but most of it comes from the years before World War I, when it was still reasonable for a thoughtful man to talk of the progress of civilization. In

America it was the time of the maturity of William James, the prime of life of Dewey, the youth of Frank Lloyd Wright; and Jespersen breathes their spirit, of the matter-of-fact, the efficient, the democratic, the promise of an industrial economy to make a decent society. In that period the "enemies" seemed to be the reactionary, unscientific, and genteel, the dead grammar of the "classics," and not, as now, the streamlined and plastic and the misuse of computers. Philosophically, there was not yet a climate of existentialism, phenomenology, and psychotherapy to criticize abstraction and goal-directed efficiency. Yet, like other great men of the time, just because of his democratic passion, his animality, and his common sense, Jespersen intuitively felt the dangers of the very rationalization that he espoused, and he created something else. James's *Varieties of Religious Experience,* Dewey's preoccupation with children, Wright's rural reconstructionism, Weber's *Protestant Ethic,* and Jespersen's aboriginal language all manifest the same unease.

3 . Poems as Complex-Words

A poem, though it may be written in a modern "analytic" language, can be usefully regarded as speaking Jespersen's aboriginal language. The analogy is fairly exact. A poem is one inseparable irregular conglomeration, chanted. The word order is likely to be twisted. The names are particularistic and anomalous. New metaphors are invented. There is use of echoic meaning and expressive natural signs. There is strong use of tone and rhythm, sometimes even meter. The syntax is manipulated more than is common, sometimes "incorrectly," to give it more meaning. The exposition of the sentence follows the speaker's exploration of the subject rather than a uniform rule. All of this is for the purpose of saying a feelingful concrete situation, rather than making discursive remarks about it.

Most of these uses are familiar in most poems and need no illustration. But let me give a couple of illustrations of deviating from the "correct" grammar, since this is more surprising in literary poets. It can be powerfully effective. Just because the grammar carries the more "metaphysical" meaning of the sentence, its deviation can ring a loud bell.

1. The Lord is my shepherd; I shall not want.
2. He maketh me to lie down in green pastures; He leadeth me beside the still waters.
3. He restoreth my soul; He leadeth me in the paths of righteousness for His name's sake.
4. Yea, though I walk through the valley of the shadow of death, I will fear no evil, for Thou art with me; Thy rod and Thy staff they comfort me.
5. Thou preparest a table before me in the presence of mine enemies; Thou anointest my head with oil; my cup runneth over.

In its English translation, this is not far from common speech in word order, and the exposition of ideas is quite logical. The rhythmic phrasing, the persistent metaphor, and the concreteness of the detail are typically poetical. But it is the grammar that is noteworthy and surprising. In verse 4, as the picture becomes dark and the tone agitated, there is a shift from "me" to "I," and then suddenly appears "Thou," instead of the expected "He." The discourse is transformed to the I and Thou of intimate prayer. As it is set up, it seems to be this change that gives the poet courage for the astonishing arrogance of verse 5, entirely different from the humble confidence of the preceding. This is a curious little poem.[3]

3. It will be noticed that I have omitted the last verse of the Twenty-Third Psalm. As a friendly literary critic—though perhaps

An even more drastic shift of grammar occurs in Wordsworth's "There Was a Boy." For the first sixteen lines of
the poem, the poet describes the boy hallooing in the
valley; he explores the subject more erratically than would
occur in prose, but he sticks to a simple past tense—"he
blew"—or a frequentative past—"they would shout." But
then appears suddenly (my italics),

> . . . when there came a pause
> Of silence such as baffled his best skill:
> Then, sometimes, in that silence, while he hung
> Listening, a gentle shock of mild surprise
> *Has carried* far into his heart the voice
> Of mountain-torrents.

The tense is so surprising that one takes it for a printer's
error and consults other editions! But there is no error.
This past continuing into the present—and we will soon
learn that the boy is dead—is Wordsworth's theory of perception and immortality, brought on by the gentle shock
of recognition. Hastily, the poem withdraws from it and
reverts to the correct sequence of past tenses—until the
crushing announcement,

> This boy was taken from his mates, and died
> In childhood. . . .
> Pre-eminent in beauty *is* the vale. . . .
>   . . . there
> A long half-hour together I *have stood*
> Mute.

(Wordsworth often modulates the tenses in this way;
for elaborate examples, cf. "With Ships the Sea was
Sprinkled Far and Nigh" or "The Solitary Reaper." He is
the greatest master of expressive syntax in English. Almost
invariably his purpose is to bring the past into an eternal

---

not as a theologian—I would have advised David to strike it. "My
cup runneth over" is too delicious not to end on.

present: "The music in my heart I bore,/Long after it was heard no more." But whatever his metaphysical intention, the poetic effect is immediacy: The *saying* of the experience is the essence of the experience that is said.)

Jespersen's thesis of the evolution of language toward the "analytic" and regular does not apply to poetry. Manipulating the grammar and twisting the word order, sophisticated modern poets converge with poets of highly inflected languages of antiquity; there is finally not much difference in gross style between Keats, Goethe, and Baudelaire, and Horace, Sappho, and (sometimes) the Psalmist. This is remarkable, as the analogy to the aboriginal language is remarkable. Much, even very much, can be explained by imitation; but why do they bother to imitate? I am not satisfied that I understand why poets, and myself as a poet, come on in this language. So let me reflect for a couple of pages on the nature of language and the purposes of poetic language.

Any language can be used for good speech by good speakers. There is no poverty-stricken language, though there may be persons or groups who are linguistically blocked for other reasons. In previous chapters I have tried to show that people make an intimate language by modifying the pronunciation, vocabulary, and grammar, and by using smiles and frowns, grunts and gestures, omitting what does not need to be said, and responding to the listener's signals as they go along. Jespersen liked to say that modern English is especially apt for easy, lively, and pointed communication, but we know that primitive languages serve, and we have no reason to believe that classical languages did not serve.

The problem in making a poem is quite different. It is to be feelingful and concrete and to take account of the listener and the situation when *there can be no recourse to non-verbal means,* when there is no respondent, and when colloquial modifications that we make in small groups would be meaningless in public discourse. A poem has to do what good speakers do, but it must do it entirely by its language.

Putting it this way, I am at once struck by the solitude of the poet. He is without actual conversation. Then he is freed from its conditions, of having to cope with the common code and meet the understanding of the hearer. He can invent any language he wants, but he tries to invent a language that "everybody" can understand. Does he have a nostalgia for a simpler speech-community where people are not solitary? Paradoxically, he uses a language that people do not talk.

He objectifies the whole conversation. This makes me think that he is projecting it from the unconscious: The conversation is a wish. In form, a poem looks very like a monologue; it *is* a monologue. But a monologue is not the same as talking to oneself. It is more like a daydream.

The language of poetry is not "poetic diction." In certain cultural conditions there may develop a guild language or constructed jargon that poets use, for instance the Greek of the Homerids or Dante's Italian. There are also the rococo excesses of so-called "Augustan" periods—which, incidentally, are unlike the plain Latin of the Augustan poets Virgil, Horace, and Ovid. And dismayed at the debasement of language in modern mass culture, many poets of the twentieth century have hit on a poetic diction, usually borrowed from the symbolists. But by and large, I agree with the major consensus of English and American critics for nearly two centuries that it is a mistake for poets to speak a guild language. It stands between them and the people; it keeps them out of colloquial contact with themselves; it puts them into frozen attitudes.

Rather, poetry comes to a special language by the following route. Poetry starts from good colloquial speech.

Common speech is cheap material available to everybody, just as the other fine arts use colored mud, rock, humming and drumming, moving the limbs, mimicking, available to everybody. Every art medium has its characteristics, but it is not much pre-formed, so it can be formed. And we use these simple media from early childhood, speaking, building with blocks, molding sand, scribbling with crayons and finger-painting, singing, dancing, putting on costumes. It is astounding how natural and few the fine arts are. Modern technology has developed highly effective artificial media, of light, sound, and engineering, but they are not simple, cheap, or childish.

Yet as soon as the poet begins to tell his individual occasion and to *live* it in language—speaking is very much his way of being in the world—he deviates from common speech. He does not deviate into further colloquialism. Indeed, he is likely to diminish the colloquial elements, of bad pronunciation, private words, ellipses and redundancies, because they are not clear. Rather, he draws on a bigger vocabulary than is common, revives old-fashioned expressions, neologizes, and becomes nice about the grammar. And especially, since he wants to live the occasion *through,* with a beginning, middle, and end—and yet remaining entirely within language!—his phrases close back on themselves and reinforce one another. He forms a complex word. The word becomes a thing.

But neither is the language of poetry a private language, an idiolect, though it is always partly an idiolect —every strong writer molds a language that works primarily for himself. But a poet finds his language mainly in the poetic tradition that he belongs to. This explains the imitation. He speaks in common with other poets not because they have a special language, but because they have all worked on the same problem—how to live it through in words. One needs help; one's desperate fellows are the community. There is no guild "poetic diction," but there is a living tradition of poets that I talk to. (They are not boring, either.) This is the essential truth in Longinus's advice to "write it for Demosthenes, write it for Plato." It is not because they set a standard, but because they understand the problem.

One could fantasize that the poetic tradition extends right back to the aboriginal language, and we never did forget how to talk it! But the realistic explanation is quite adequate: Human beings are so busy and ingenious; then consider the effect of the concerted effort of a gifted group over generations and centuries, and indeed millennia, in devising and refining literary expressions, not losing touch with one another.

In my own case, which I suppose is usual, I feel entirely free to invent versification, grammar, or vocabulary, and sometimes I have to, to say my say. Nobody hinders me from composing as I please, and in our society there is even a premium on novelty. Yet if I can remember devices and styles from the poems that I know that are roughly adequate to my needs, I eagerly seize on them and modify them like *our* common code. Naturally, a poet who has much newer things to say than I have has to invent more language to say it; and an unsophisticated poet, who does not know the traditional code so well, has to invent more, usually clumsily, sometimes beautifully and freshly.

Besides, traditional verse forms that have had a great history usually have a basis in nature. For dramatic poetry, Greek iambic-trimeter, French alexandrine, and English blank verse roughly take up a breath. (Reciters of Homeric hexameters must have had good breathing, like singers. Later imitators, like Virgil, are just being grand.) The Italian sonnet, which seems to be a pure artifact, has had an astonishing success in every Western language. I think it is because both its tightness and its asymmetry roughly imitate the asymmetrical motion of a kind of reflective thought: examples and rule, rule and example, if . . . then, circumstances and a wish, etc. From the example of Villon, the implicated rimes of ballades have been used to bind together itemized lists; whereas the fourteener stanzas of ballads have narrated episodic stories to a repeating tune. Such contents, of course, could be said, and have been said, in other verse forms and in prose. Yet if a form is roughly apt, a few successful uses of it can create a traditional expectation of it; writers imitate it and critics and audiences consider it peculiarly "appropriate." It is then taught in academic courses as if it had some special nature as the language of "poetry."

A poet promptly modifies the traditional form, and it is an advantage to have a norm to modify. For instance, Milton's pentameters have 3, 2, or 4 beats, depending on the speed needed to build up feeling through his paragraphs, which are his real periods or conglomerations. In his sonnets, he either impatiently breaks in before the boundary of the octave ("On His Blindness"), or he overflows the boundary with fullness of thought ("Massacre in Piemont," "Cromwell"), or he civilly abides by the boundary ("Cyriack Skinner"), or he goes right past it in order to isolate one terrible last line ("Deceased Wife").

Finally, there is what might be called the religious meaning of poetical language. Poetry as a life wager. Creating *another* world, instead of living this one.

In the aboriginal language, we saw, there might be a blurring between lexicon and grammar, between denotative names and meanings given by formal devices. Likewise, in some primitive languages there is a very large number of acceptable sounds, clicks, explosive noises, and musical tones, and there might be a blurring between what are words and what are mere echoes and exclamations. Both these blurrings occur, in a more sophisticated way, in

poems. But in poems there is an even more important ambiguity, an ambiguity of semantics: What is language and
what is being talked about? This is usually posed as the
question, "Does poetry mean anything?" or "Is the 'meaning' of a poem just the poem itself?" or "Can a poem be
paraphrased?" Let me repeat from previous chapters some
passages that bear on this question:

> All speech is assertive. . . . Poetry is also assertive, but
> it does not say sentences about reality and sometimes
> does not use the common code. Rather, it goes about
> the business more directly, by tying down more reality
> in its complicated structures than is possible in ordinary
> sentences and by trying to make the poem itself more
> like a real thing.
>
> Poets have rarely regarded their speech as communica-
> tion, but usually as a physical thing. In classical literary
> theory, poems are imitations; and the discussion of
> imitations is usually how to make them "like whole
> animals," as Aristotle put it, self-subsistent and inter-
> nally coherent.
>
> Speaking is such that there comes to be a world made
> of signs. Meantime these same signs are functional for
> biological and community survival, personal well-being,
> and intellectual growth. And we cannot simply sort
> out the two aspects, for the functional use of words
> requires that people believe in their meanings, and
> this belief is in the speaker and hearer—it is not in the
> relation of the signs and the designates.

The words that are parts of a poem are not nonsense
syllables. The poet believes they have meaning, and he
wants to use just these words and not others. Nor does he
do this just to "express himself"; he is making a public
statement, and he feels the strongest responsibility—it is his
only responsibility—to make the statement "clear," though
hardly ever to a particular audience, even when it is a

declaration of love. By this activity he lives through, and brings into the public forum, an occasion that is important to him; and he does this as a human being, he is not assuming the role of "being a poet." In short, all parts of the discourse are real, real speech, except that, *unlike* in the aboriginal language, the poem has no real referent, it is a complex-word that closes on itself. A poet simply doesn't care if what he says is true, at least as propositions are true.[4]

Also, poetry is not rhetoric. An audience that is not a particular audience is not a respondent at all. Thus, the only test of the relevance of his poem is whether or not he carries it off. Does it hang together? Does it have magnitude or is it trivial? Is it interesting or boring? Is it believable? But poetic credibility is *not* a semantical relation; it depends on how the poet manages the words. A poem lacks verisimilitude—*"incredulus odi,"* as Horace says—not because its propositions are fantastic—most poetic sentences are anyway lies, fictions, platitudes, or exaggerations—but because it does not carry the hearer along.

What an extraordinary psychotic characteristic of human nature to need to reconstruct the world in this way! And sometimes to manage to reconstruct it and make it stick.

On the one hand, one thinks of Flaubert and the farm family: "They have the right of it." On the other, there was Beethoven unbelievably miserable, but he must have been something like happy during those hours of exploding energy and long song when he was not there.

4. As a poet, I like to compose with accurate observations and true propositions, but this is not to inform or persuade anybody. It is because true propositions lie heavier on the page—I can't just push them around; it's like carving wood rather than modeling clay.

CHAPTER IX

Literary Process

1

But whether poetry or prose, statements in literary works are also taken seriously as *about* something; they are quoted by philosophers and men of letters are invited to confer with experts as if they had something useful to contribute. They are not scientific statements. They are grounded in something. But in what? It is not exactly evidence. What kind of statement *is* it that men of letters make? What is their warrant for making it? I think the warrant is in the literary process itself.

There are innumerable books on works of literature and the lives of their authors, and there are many books on the philosophy of art. But to my surprise, I cannot think of a comprehensive study of the literary process—what it is to write books—drawn from what men of letters do. Let me spell out its characteristics and compare them with other disciplines, and see if they add up to a warrant for stating anything meaningful and true. As in the rest of this book, I will try to stay with things that are *prima facie*.

Like everybody else, a writer has a day-to-day life; but unlike any scientist or almost any professional, a writer's daily life and course of life are relevant to his special work and may at any time appear in his sentences. He may say, "My experience has been that . . ." or "For instance, yesterday I had a quarrel with my daughter and . . ." I can think of only pastoral theology and psychotherapy as professions where this would not be out of place, since they deal face-to-face with their clients and speak *ad hominem*. If a social scientist uses such sentences, he is at once identified as a writer (and dismissed).

A writer certainly does not deal *ad hominem* with his unknown readers; yet his readers may take it as if he does and send him letters and so forth.

A writer objectively observes, in this being like a scientist. His method is best compared, in this respect, to natural history or anthropology. A young writer is well advised to learn the geography, botany, and animals—a good model is Hardy—as well as the people and institutions. A writer's method is naturalist; he does not intervene experimentally nor with questionnaires, though like other naturalists, he may station himself to notice what he needs to know.

But then, unlike scientific naturalists, he focuses on the individual case with its unique characteristics, like a painter painting just this scene, or a physician treating just this patient.

He brings together his personal life and the objective subject matter, and the general class and the individual case.

Writers rely heavily on memory (the mother of the Muses) of both their own biographies and the cultural tradition. Only law, philosophy, and history itself draw as much on records of the past decades, centuries, and millennia. The faculty of bringing together memory and learning with present observation and spontaneous impulse is again a remarkable service for human beings. Man is the animal who makes himself and the one who is made by his culture. Literature repeats the meaning and revives the spirit of past makings, so they are not a dead weight, by using them again in a making that is occurring now.

I would not like to distinguish literature from philosophy, if we take philosophy to be the collecting of wide-flung concrete experience—in principle all the experience there is—and saying what is central in it. There are various methods of philosophizing, for instance logical analysis, phenomenological description, grounding and harmonizing the different sciences. Literature could be called philosophizing by making and experimenting with language.

Writers are linguistic analysts and know the folk wisdom and superstition that exist in common vocabulary and grammar. As General Semanticists, they are critical of the rhetoric of the street, the mass media, and official institutions. They understand, more than most people, what cannot be said, what is not being said though it ought to be, what is verbalized experience, and what is mere words. They can detect when there is really an idea and an argument rather than a cloud of phrases. They can date a passage and show a forgery. As psychologists of language they are sensitive to how people come on when they talk or write, the ploys they use, and the postures they strike. They can hear the personal character that is expressed in habits of syntax, and the personal inhibition or freedom that is told by the breathing and rhythm of sentences and the quality of metaphor. They can judge the clarity or confusion or spurious clarity in an exposition. They are sociologists of language and can recognize the social background in vocabulary, pronunciation, and routine formulas.

At the same time as they know all this, however, in their own writing they must let their speech come spontaneously; it is free speech, though they monitor it critically, as we shall discuss later. It pursues tangents that they did not plan, produces metaphors that surprise them, uses word order with an emphasis they did not know they had, argues in a way to contradict their theses, and says ideas that they themselves judge to be unpolitical or immoral. But they do not censor or control this wildness; they do their best to assimilate it and keep going. Sometimes the whole must be torn up because it has fallen apart. For writers, these wildnesses are like the phenomena that must be saved by the empirical scientist. There are different ideologies to explain the necessity not to control —it is inspiration, it is unconscious contents emerging; the unconscious contents are the return of individual hangups or they are imagos from the depths, the spontaneous is the voice of the people or universal man speaking through the writer. Whatever the ideology, a writer writes at the boundary of what he knows.

Not to censor is an act of moral will, a commitment. At some point early in his career a young writer must come to it, like a kind of Hippocratic oath. If he can think something, he will say it; if it says itself, he will not strike it; if he can write it, he will publish it. The writing does not belong to "himself." [1] The refusal of censorship and self-

1. An interesting problem arises with regard to copyright. In principle, what is authentically written is not a commodity bought and paid for, but is in the public domain like air and water and natural growth. Yet as a citizen, I object to my writing being exploited for somebody's profit. So I try to set the following conditions: If anybody wants to reprint my writing for non-commercial purposes, they can do so gratis; if the State wants to use it, they must give me safeguards; if a commercial enterprise wants to use it, they must pay the going market price.

censorship is, of course, essential for the use of writing against lying and oppressive regimes; but it also makes a writer a thorn in the side of his own political cause: He gets nice about the slogans; he can't say the half-truth; he states the case of the opposition better than is convenient; and so forth. A writer might be a fine citizen in a perfect community, to which he would lend animation; but he is an unreliable ally—he is "unrealistic"—in actual politics.

The spontaneity, the free origination, of writing is one aspect of a writer's disinterestedness; he does not will it, but he is present with it. The other aspect is as follows.

He writes it *through,* from the beginning through the middle to the end. This is a writer's chief moral virtue; it is an act of will and often requires a lot of fortitude. It is what distinguishes a writer from a dilettante. A young writer is well advised to start on things he can finish and not get bogged down in long novels. By finishing, you learn the habits that work for you and can then set up a bigger structure.

To make a whole work, each sentence follows from the sentence before with "literary probability" and advances the whole, until nothing more follows. (I will return to the meaning of "literary probability.") In the course of a fairly long work, there are bound to be impasses. The writer must backtrack and choose other alternatives, observe more, and sometimes have bad headaches till he invents something. Here lies the distinction between a good writer and a bad writer. A good writer does not fake it and try to make it appear, to himself or the reader, that there is a coherent and probable whole when there isn't. If the writer is on the right track, however, things fall serendipitously into place; his sentences prove to have more meaning and formative power than he expected; he has new insights; and the book "writes itself."

At the end of this process, somehow, the finished work

will have been worth doing. If it is a long poem, it will have the kind of meaning that poems have, that I spoke of in the last chapter. If it is a prose essay, it will say something true about its subject matter.[2]

This last is, of course, simply an act of faith, but it is no different in kind from the faith of all who work at the boundary of the unknown—the faith of a physician that, if he pursues his method, nature will heal the patient; or the faith of an empirical scientist that, if he pursues his method, the nature of things will reveal a secret; or, for that matter, the faith of a child who runs across a field and the ground supports him. If they fail, they do not give up the method, because they have no alternative way of being. When they succeed, they get a passing satisfaction and go on to another work.

Finally, there is an odd and revealing unilateral contract that a writer makes with his readers. Some writing, of course, like a political tract, an entertainment, or a popularization, is aimed at a particular audience and always keeps them in mind; but much serious writing, perhaps most, is written for no particular audience; and much fiction and poetry for none at all. Nevertheless, the writer is always under an obligation to make it "clear." He will explain references that an ordinary literate reader is not

2. Schopenhauer or Nietzsche—I no longer remember which; either is possible because both were snappish and down-to-earth—advises looking first at the last chapter and asking *"Was will der Mensch?"* ("What's the man after?"). He is after where he ends up. But has he *gone* there? If so, you have to go the way with him. My own usual experience is that I do start out with him frankly on his way; but somewhere along he fakes something, or he doesn't know something that he ought to know, and then I find it hard to continue. My experience also is that one can usually easily recognize the writer who is really in there pitching, suffering, doing his best, finding new things—at least new to himself—and not just working a sewing machine. To him one allows any number of mistakes and gaps.

likely to know; he will fill out the argument; he will avoid private or clique information, even though his ideal audience would hardly need such help. But "clear" does not mean easily comprehensible—consider Mallarmé, an exceedingly clear and logical writer, but who cannot sacrifice the conciseness, texture, and immediacy of his style just to be easily understood by readers, so you have to figure it out like a puzzle. My opinion is that, in most cases, the writer is not thinking of a reader at all; he makes it "clear" as a contract with *language*. Since it is the essence of speech to have a hearer—even though he intends no hearer—the correct use of speech is to be clear.

Let us go back to the question I started with. How do these traits and powers of literary writing add up to a warrant to make true statements, in the sense that scientific statements are true? They don't. *But there is no alternative.* There is no other discourse but literature that is subjective and objective, general and concrete, spontaneous and deliberate, and that, though it is just thinking aloud, gives so much attention to language, our chief communication.

Philosophers are mistaken to quote literary texts as if they provided another line of proof, a special kind of evidence. As a writer, I do not judge that I provide evidence. But I do go through the literary process to produce the text.

Men of letters have definite virtues. They do not wear blinders. They are honest and do not omit the seamy or awkward side. They are intolerant of censorship and skeptical of authority. They work hard to write it through. They disinterestedly lose themselves in what they do and are innocently in love with the product.

But it is not so definite what is the use of their ethic. They are not committed, like scientists, to find confirmable and replicable truth. Politically, they are usually inept at finding ways to realize what they advocate. They are not trustworthy as pedagogues or curers of souls.

Perhaps, in the social division of labor, they are the group to whom it is assigned to make sense. One is reminded of Nestor, the orator of the *Iliad*. Nestor's honeyed speech at no time dissuaded the Greeks from their infatuation, but it was no doubt a good thing for them to go to their doom with open eyes.

Why would anyone behave as writers do? A scholar making a comprehensive study of the literary process would finally have to try to ground it in depth psychology and religion, for it is peculiar. The best essay in this direction has been Otto Rank's *Art and Artist*. Rank points out, among other things, that writers and artists try to find meaning in experience, or impose meaning on it, in order to nullify death; but they are forced to feed on fame instead, since they do not find proof. Our scholar would also have to ask about the political community that needs and (stingily) supports this disposition. My own hunch is that the process of literature is inherent in the nature of language; it is a sophisticated result of the verbal doubling of the world that we are thrown to as speaking animals. Since we cannot avoid this duplicity, we domesticate it as literature. If so, we can expect it in every culture, though not necessarily to the degree that we know it.

2 . What Is "Literary"?

Painters disparage a painting as too "literary," meaning that it tells a story or depends for its effect on the sitter's expression or the picturesqueness of a landscape, whereas the right values of painting are composition, planes, color, texture, the action of the painter. Similarly, musicians object that a score too "literally" follows a program.

Their way of putting it is mistaken. What they call "literary" is common experience; life is full of interesting incidents, characteristic faces, striking landscapes, moments of passion and conflict. Artists in any medium—words, paint, tones, or body movements—will imitate common experience, whether or not they mean to be abstract. Indeed, the more abstract the effort, the easier it can be read as a projection of character, like the choices in a Rorschach test. A passage of music, being a rhythmic motion of perceptions, will inevitably express feeling.

There is a related question that is more interesting: It is claimed that some aspects of common experience are better imitated in one medium and some in another—the face in painting, the thought in words, the feeling in musical tones. This seems to be plausible, and it has the powerful authority of Lessing's *Laocoön,* that the sculptor must catch the still point. But the bother with such *a priori* proscription of what cannot be well done is that some inventive son of a gun will carry it off successfully tomorrow.

The real objection that the painters and musicians are making is that the "content" of the work is not merged in the medium. It has an organization of its own that is irrelevant to, and distracts from, the pictorial and musical values. Exactly the same lack of artistry can occur in putting the "content" of experience into the medium of literature. The means of literature are naming, alluding to, defining, syllogism and enthymeme, speed and succession of propositions, coordination and subordination of clauses, balance of sentences, metrical rhythm and other rhythm, metaphor, individual terms, specific terms, generic terms, colloquial and learned words, (in English) Saxon

and French and Latin words, direct and indirect discourse,
paradox and irony, period and stanza and paragraph, tenses
and moods and voices of verbs, etc., etc. These are very
extensive means—it is a grand medium—but they are also
quite specific to language as the medium. Much of classical
literary criticism (and my own book *The Structure of
Literature*) consists of nothing but discussion of how to
combine these possibilities into whole works. Let me give
one obvious but important example: In a temporal medium like speech, we can directly convey an action just
by letting the sequence of the sentences follow the moments of the action, but it is always an embarrassment to
present a fixed habit, e.g. character, without just talking
about it. A usual literary device to cope with this problem
is to accumulate a series of like incidents or behaviors, and
"character" is what they have in common; the expectation
is that the next behavior will be like, the "character" will
be "consistent." It is then a source of "probability" in the
plot.[3]

The idea of structural criticism is to show how experience can be re-created in the medium of words, and then
we discuss the poem as words. Aristotle's *Poetics* is mainly
about how a serious action that ends in a downfall can be
told as a complex tragic plot; "serious," "action," "downfall" all end up as combinations of literary means, words.
In *The Structure of Literature,* I extend the same method
to other human destinies, states, and feelings. (I do not
think that this nominalistic mode of criticism is the only
useful one, any more than it is in linguistics. But in both
cases it has power.)

3. If I may make a dumb-bunny suggestion: A chief reason why
logicians, from Aristotle on, are eager to stretch out essences into
definitions, e.g. by giving genus and differentia, is to be able to get
speech in motion for their discourse, e.g. to syllogize. If we painted
philosophy instead of writing it, essences would not be defined.
Definition belongs to language.

Recently, a clamorous attack on literature has been coming from the champions of multi-media. In my opinion, it is nonsensical. They say that writing, and indeed all speech, is "linear"—it pays out its meanings one after another like signals on an unrolling tape. But in fact, speech can be amazingly contrapuntal, more so even than orchestral music with all its voices and timbres. In colloquial speech, the phonetics, grammar, and lexicon can simultaneously have meaning, either reinforcing or shading one another, and to these we must add non-verbal signs and attending to the respondent. Writing, which is more deliberate speech, lacks the non-verbal and the respondent, but it adds contrapuntal voices, like a system of metaphor, systematic irony, allegory, subordination of clauses in the framework of an independent clause—consider a paragraph of Proust. In poetry it is usual for three systems of rhythm to be heard at the same time: the meter, the beats of phrasing, and the period or paragraph. Good colloquial conversation or the complex-word of a poem can keep globally in touch with almost every aspect of a situation.

Speech rises from within people; they reach out to say it or to hear it, even when they are reading. My observation is that people are rather passive to multi-media. Multimedia have their own quality, of surrounding and sometimes penetrating, but they are not a substitute for saying. It is possible—I doubt it—that future technological and cultural changes may put writing and reading out of business, but other media will not then do the same job as words. It is hard, if at all possible, for non-verbal means to syllogize, define, state class inclusion, subordinate, say a subjunctive or even imperative or interrogative, to distinguish direct and indirect discourse, to say "I-Thou" or "It," etc., etc. Film, music, and space arrangements have to use indirect means to communicate these simple things. On this subject, people like Marshall McLuhan don't know what they're talking about, though they have other useful things to say. If they would try to write through a book, they would have to make more sense. A written argument won't hang together unless it copes with at least the obvious objections. Putting in a picture doesn't help.

Nevertheless, there is certainly a natural drive toward mixed media. Brute experience is given in a global combination of seeing, hearing, touching, kinesthesia, common sensibles,[4] and including locomotion, speaking, and desire; so artists are bound to try to reconstruct the combination. Every primitive culture combines words, melody, and rhythm in songs and dances, and dresses up the dancers with costumes, and arranges and decorates the setting for the song and dance. Richard Wagner's effort for "total theater" seems to be a valid ideal.

In my opinion, it is an artistic mistake to surround and engulf people, from outside, with artificial impressions. In such a process, especially the literary medium, words, must get trivialized or forced out, for the hearer of words must have a psychological space to interpret the words, to respond to them as meaningful sentences; but only shouts, slogans, and traffic-signals are loud enough to be heard in a busy esthetic surface. Artaud and the multi-media people are quite correct in their judgment that literature stands in the way of the engulfing multimedia effect. But it ought to be possible to proceed the other way, from inward outward. Thus, in a song, if the words and thought are fairly simple, they can be heard along with the melody and rhythm of the accompaniment; their feeling is powerfully reinforced by the music, which soon takes over in its own structures—the final effect of

4. "Common sensibles" is Aristotle's useful term for particular percepts that may be given by the combined action of different sense organs; e.g. we may perceive that a sight and a sound are simultaneous or successive.

an art-song, if not a ballad or folk song, is musical and not literary.

(Art-songs are a curious genre. The human voice is probably the most flexible and interesting of musical instruments, as well as being the most available, and this is surely a major reason why composers of art-songs write for it. But they then seem to think that the human voice should be saying *something*, not just nonsense syllables, so they have to find texts to set. Most good poems, however, get in the way of the music, are too complicated.)

In theater, the actors start with words but, especially at the climactic moments, the meaning of the words is completed by non-verbal overt actions and the blocking of the whole scene. As usually in ordinary life, the words are no longer the chief part of the experience. In plays of Racine, as I have pointed out previously, the *coup de théâtre* consists not even of an overt gesture but the mere entrance of a character on the scene. A wonderful example of total theater is the conclusion of *Walküre*: Wotan calls up Loge with words, but it is the ensuing spectacle and its music that send us; the words, and the characters themselves, are transcended. We *are* engulfed. To be sure, this is one crashingly successful case among plenty of failures.

CHAPTER X

Literary Style as Hypothesis

1

Return now to the thesis of Benjamin Whorf, that the language determines the metaphysics of the tribe and what people can think. We saw that this formulation was too sweeping. Language is checked by non-verbal experience. Language itself is plastic and says new things when necessary. People do manage to communicate across the barrier of culture and language; we do get something out of Homer. In the problems of philosophy, we can think away the language of previous thinkers and still usually find a real problem for ourselves.

If we put Whorf's thesis in a more modest form, it is more rewarding. People use language, they are not determined by it; but when they do use it—and by the language they choose—they focus their experience and define and limit their thoughts. A style of speech is an hypothesis about how the world is. A good style, colloquial or literary, is one that is adequate to cope with a wide and necessary range of experience. It proves itself as a way of being, it does not break down, it is believable.

This view is similar to the newer philosophy of linguistic analysis that has developed out of linguistic positivism. Instead of treating popular metaphysics as nonsense in which people are stuck and to which prophylaxis must be applied, linguistic analysis takes common speech as a repository of vast empirical experience of curious matters by the community, just as the Common Law is the embodied wisdom of the Anglo-Saxon people (such as it is). The philosophical problem is to decipher exactly what is being said; judging by colloquial sentences, what do people *mean* when they say: "mind," "cause," "responsibility," "good," "bad," and so forth? Literary style is a convenient object for this kind of analysis. Common language is a static, encrusted, and random relic of philosophizing; in style we can see hypothesizing in action and trying to be coherent.

2

In ancient texts, perhaps because of distance so that the gross features stand out, style seems to provide an hypothesis of the nature of things not for an individual speaker but for the entire culture. So let us start with the most ancient style available.

An ancient Egyptian, says Henri Frankfort in *Ancient Egyptian Religion,* had "the conviction that his universe was a world without change," and this idea pervaded every institution, including the literature. Unlike contemporary Babylonian and Hebrew works, which are storytelling and historical, there is no narrative or epical treatment of

Egyptian myths. Instead, the *achieved* result of the history, story, or conflict is cast as a static hymn.

The literary problem is the opposite of the one mentioned in the last chapter, how to represent a permanent trait like "character" in a moving medium like speech; here it is how to stop the motion of speech in representing a moving action. Thus, the action of the death and succession of Osiris is told as follows:

> Beneficent Isis, that protected her brother, that sought for him without wearying, and took no rest till she found him.
>
> She that afforded him shade with her feathers, and with her wings created air. She that cried aloud for joy and brought her brother to land.
>
> She that revived the faintness of the Weary One, that took in his seed and provided an heir, that suckled the child in solitude; that brought him, when his arm was strong, into the Hall of Geb . . .

Obviously the story is being told, but the message, "the unchanging relation between worshipper and god," is conveyed by never allowing an independent verb.[1] (I have no idea how this syntax is read into the hieroglyphics, but I am sure that Frankfort's rendering must be accurate.)

The battle of the Sun and the dark Serpent is always recounted after the victory has been won; the vanquished lies there in the passive voice and in past participles, in

---

1. Those who know the Passover *Haggadah* will recognize the same device in the hymn "Dayenu": "If He had brought us out of Egypt, it would have been enough for us. . . . If He had divided the Red Sea, it would have been enough for us. Etc." So the whole story is told in detail, but it is not told as a story.

For a masterly, flexible way of achieving the same static sculptural effect, there is no better example than Pindar. He does it by continually referring back to himself as the admiring panegyrist and by stopping the narration of the athletic event, which could hardly bear much retelling, with digressions about the victor's family, etc.

front of the triumphant Boat of the Sun. Similarly, there are dramatic impersonations, like *The Mystery Play of the Succession* at inaugurals—in spite of all, the rulers do die —but nothing is ever told except

> the perennial truth that Horus succeeds Osiris. The gods appear and speak once more the words they spoke "the first time." Thus the unavoidable change which takes place in the state is equated with the archetypal relation between Osiris and his son and successor.

There is more than a hint of the same procedure in those remarkable passages in Genesis that are transparently retellings of the same episode in each generation. (Thomas Mann handles them deliciously in his books about Joseph—for to repeat a behavior mechanically is essentially comic.)

In Egyptian lyrical poems, each stanza begins with an unvarying formula that dictates what the feeling is about. One is reminded of the refrain in folk ballads that comes at the end of the stanzas. In the ballads, the story rapidly develops and the feeling grows among the hearers, who presumably sing the refrain. But where the formula occurs at the beginning of each stanza, it seems to me, the effect would be to hold the feeling in check.

But a good style must be able to say how the world is, and how can such a static style possibly be adequate to experience that contains so many transient occurrences and particular details that do not warrant such splendid fixity? The Egyptian answer is simple indeed: Such things are dryly chronicled and tacked on like a laundry list or jottings in a desk diary, e.g. "Year 23, first month of the third season . . . on the sixteenth day he arrived at the city of Yehem"; "Statement of the harvest which was brought to his majesty from the fields of Megiddo . . . 208,200 . . . fourfold heket measures of grain." The text may then continue with its formal hymn of praise.

The most interesting of Frankfort's examples is the short story, "The Eloquent Shepherd." This begins with a charming account of the Shepherd coming to the capital, in a folksy narrative style with plenty of action, not unlike a naturalistic ballad. This proves that the Egyptians *could* write in such a manner, as we would guess anyway from the naturalistic wall paintings. But then, surprisingly to modern ears, the text turns into a static manual of Court flattery, as the Shepherd appeals his case to the Pharaoh, and this proves to be the point of the story and no doubt the reason for its survival. What is remarkably indicated by such an example is not that the culture determines the style, but that the writer's style determines how the culture is to be taken. He *chooses* the cultural imperative and says it; he *can* speak otherwise.

Among ourselves, a wonderful example of the static style is *Adonais*. Shelley makes the poem not move and not move, for almost too long; and then it moves—to the explanation of why it does not move: "The One remains, the many change and pass." And the monotonous Spenserian stanzas have begun to roar like an organ point. At this moment the poem is beyond praise. *Adonais* is another one of those masterpieces that, it seems, could not possibly work because the set-up is so crazy.

3

An elaborate study of our theme is Erich Auerbach's *Mimesis: The Representation of Reality in Western Literature*. Auerbach begins with the justly famous gambit of contrasting Homer and Genesis as the opposite extremes in the origin of Western style—a dominant idea of the book is to show the enriching influence of the Judaeo-Christian tradition upon Classical realism.

The passages chosen are the recognition of Odysseus's scar by his old nurse and the Sacrifice of Isaac, and Auerbach summarizes the contrast as follows:

> On the one hand [in Homer], fully externalized description, uniform illumination, uninterrupted connection, free expression, all events in the foreground, displaying unmistakable meanings, few elements of historical development and of psychological perspective. On the other hand [in Genesis], certain parts brought into high relief, others left obscure, abruptness, suggestive influence of the unexpressed, "background" quality, multiplicity of meanings and the need for interpretation, universal-historical claims, development of the concept of the historically becoming, and preoccupation with the problematic.

Thus, when the old nurse recognizes the scar, Homer at once tells us how, when, and where Odysseus got it, on a visit to his grandfather, who his grandfather was, the welcoming banquet, going to sleep and waking and starting out on the hunt for the boar, the hunt, Odysseus wounded and recovering, till he finally returns to Ithaca, his parents' anxious questions. In the case of Abraham, on the other hand, we are told: "God did tempt Abraham and said to him, Abraham! and he said, Behold, here I am." But where are the speakers? is Abraham in Beersheba? in his tent? what is he doing when the summons comes? is he on his knees? and where is God? where is He speaking from, the heights or the depths? None of this is told.

This is a fair reading of the passages, and it is evident that the styles come from different worlds. But I do not exactly agree with Auerbach on how those worlds *are* for their authors. He shows that the styles are hypotheses, but (in my opinion) he does not hit the right hypotheses, and the reason is worth exploring. He does not take into account, or take into account enough, what it means for them to be *telling*, telling stories, rather than acting in some other way. The Greeks *were* clear about many things, and one of the things was that the world of free saying, whether in poetry or science, was not the same as the world of action, passion, suffering, and confusion. Whereas for various reasons, the writers—or the Writer—of Genesis did not distinguish telling from other doing so precisely.

Auerbach finds that Homer's world is entirely in the present; everything is sensuously perceptible; the persons have no subjectivity. Indeed, it seems to be the perfect dream of a behaviorist psychologist. For instance, the long story about how Odysseus got the scar is not introduced as a subjective recollection of Odysseus, but only at the moment of overt behavior, when the nurse sees it. So according to Auerbach, the Greek characters have no biographical depth and no unconscious. They are well rounded, not cartoons, but they have no past and they do not really grow or change in crisis.

But it is simpler to take Homer's foreground style psychologically at face value, with its uniform illumination and free excursions: It is the style of healthy perception without anxiety. The foreground figures are sharp and bright, the closure is good, the background is empty and untroubled, there are no repressed contents—in the *author* —threatening to return. The leisurely excursions, like the story of the scar or the long Homeric similes that leave the narrative and return to it, are exactly analogous to the best Rorschach responses that expatiate on significant details without losing sense of the whole. All this, however, is under the conditions of reciting a poem to an audience (or reading a Rorschach card). Under other conditions, the very same people, both poet and audience, have a different kind of experience that is not *said,* certainly not recited or written, namely the Mysteries, in which the dark, the cosmic, the problematic and irrational hold sway. To say it like Nietzsche: In the style of good conscience, the literary is Apollonian; the Dionysian is not the subject of epic recitation, though it may have its own individual and choral outcries.

Nor are the Homeric characters without biographical past. Auerbach takes them out of their cultural context. But their biographies existed in the general legendary knowledge of them rather than in the brief action of the *Iliad* or the adventure story of the *Odyssey,* where persons are narrated as they are, as they *have* become. As if to correct Auerbach, Aristotle makes this point explicitly in commenting on Oedipus's incredible ignorance of the facts of Laius's death: "It is outside the play," say Aristotle.[2] As I like to remind fellow pacifists, the heroes of the two Homeric epics were draft dodgers who used, though unsuccessfully, two of our current strategems to avoid going to an idiotic war. Odysseus pretended to be crazy and about to plow up his son. Achilles put on a dress and hid among the girls. And Achilles, at least, certainly changes in crisis. At the climax of the *Iliad,* he is utterly transformed into a supernatural being, looming like a demi-god. The whole scene is suffused with amazement—the horse talks, the Scamander River fights—the surrealism is astounding—that is, the background is so empty and the narrative so free that the psychotic contents of dream can shine in the foreground as of equal realism with the rest. But though Achilles is ecstatic, he is not "out of character," any more than Oedipus at Colonus; a key topic of the legend is whether Achilles is

2. Incidentally, Aristotle is wrong about the particular instance. In my opinion, Sophocles gives his characters plenty of "unconsciousness," and Oedipus is "ignorant" because he wants to be. (Cf. *The Structure of Literature,* p. 38.)

immortal, and now he has given up on life and he has a
new shield made by Vulcan.

By contrast, an unfriendly critic of Genesis could say
that the style is simply neurotic; its authors were sexually
repressed priests; the characters are all messed up by their
superstition of the authoritarian Jehovah, and the meanings are multiple because they have ambivalent feelings;
the history of interpretation is the melancholy Judaeo-
Christian tradition, sick and spiteful through and through.
My bother with *this* critique is that the style of Genesis
is not neurotic at all, but exceptionally vigorous and even
ruthless. There is no evidence that the ancient Hebrews
were sexually repressed. In the Nietzschean sense, Genesis
is quite as healthily "callous" as Homer.

Auerbach is much better on Genesis than on the
Greeks, but again, I think, he is too complicated. He takes
two different tacks in explaining the style. First, the com-
pilers were historians, practiced in telling the later epoch
of Samuel and the kings; when they wrote up the earlier
folklore, they did not resort to legend but stuck to the
sparseness of chronicle and the arbitrariness, the lack of
philosophic plot, of actual history. This explanation does
cast light on much of Genesis: the filled-out genealogies,
the namings of places, many of the mundane incidents,
e.g. Abraham bought a cave from the Hittite and was
subsequently buried there. But it is not impressive precisely for a mysterious passage like the Sacrifice on Moriah.
An historian *would* say whether the voice came to Abraham
at Beer-sheba; and he would make *some* kind of tangible
connection—perhaps to account for a marker—between
this episode and the real world. Despite Auerbach, the
story does have something of the timelessness, the isolation,
of a ballad.

Secondly, says Auerbach, these historians are compiling

a peculiar history; it is the history of the Israelites, but it is also the working out of God's plan for them. Everything happens on two planes. The mixing of these two basic histories accounts for the distinct stamp of individuality of the characters, their humiliation and elevation, their objective fate and subjective faith and so forth.

Surely, it would be simpler to explain a story like the Sacrifice by saying that Genesis is the history of *God,* not of the Israelites as such. Then the sparseness and darkness are in the nature of the case. The Israelites come into the narrative to the extent that they are His chosen people; from time to time he intervenes to keep them in line; because He is hidden, these moments are all the evidence the historian has. This was, of course, the notion of sacred history of Karl Barth, and it seems to me to explain better the abruptness and vigor of stories like the Sacrifice, and also to follow the text closer. It is God who initiates the actions: "God created the heavens and earth"; "God did tempt Abraham." We can't fill out His conditions and motives because we don't know them. It seems to me that Auerbach projects back onto the early story the endless interpretations of the "Judaeo-Christian tradition" and its presumptuous theodicy. But the basic tradition of the text is that it is Revealed; the writers are writing God's doings.

If the writers were seriously giving the history of the human persons on two planes, they could hardly avoid telling Abraham's human reaction—towering rage—at the realization that he has been "tested" or "tempted," that God has been playing games. But if it is simply God's story, no further account is needed; what else, so to speak, would one expect? As Barth puts it, the subject of the history is volcanic fire; the evidence is only the burnt-out volcanoes.

4

Leaving these ancient styles, let me jump to a famous modern style—Ernest Hemingway's—where the lineaments of the individual artist are apparent, and yet, of course, a cultural meaning is also said.

It is a passive style. The characters, including the narrator, are held off in such a way—"alienated," as Brecht puts it—that they influence nothing; events happen to them. The actions that they initiate—the story consists entirely of actions that they initiate—do not add up to actualizing them; it is one thing after another. Yet neither do the actions betray and doom them, as in ancient stories of Fate, for that would impart a meaning, a tragic meaning, to the world. Rather, the events turn out to be happenings.

Needless to say, the passivity of people in contemporary society, with its high technology and centralized organization, has been the prevailing theme of naturalistic fiction for over a century. But Hemingway takes this theme at a deeper level. His stories are located in non-industrial settings, often in fairly primitive places, and they are about activities that are even spectacularly individualistic and active: dangerous sports, smuggling, soldiers on the loose. The characters come on with a heavy preponderance of active verbs. And the effect is passive. Unlike the naturalists who show how men are puppets of the institutions, and *by* showing it inject their own activity, often political, into the prose, Hemingway contrives by his style, by what he tells and what he avoids telling, to show that happening-to-one is the nature of things. (Psychoanalytically, the passivity has been internalized.)

Here are two passages from *The Sun Also Rises,* published in 1926 when Hemingway was twenty-eight. The first is the end of a description, similar to others in the book. The characters have driven up a high mountain and it is cold.

> The bus levelled down onto the straight line of road that ran to Burguete. We passed a crossroads and crossed a bridge over a stream. The houses of Burguete were along both sides of the road. There were no side-streets. We passed the church and the school-yard, and the bus stopped. We got down and the driver handed down our bags and the rod-case. A carabineer in his cocked hat and yellow leather cross-straps came up.
>
> "What's in there?" he pointed to the rod-case.
>
> I opened it and showed him. He asked to see our fishing-permits and I got them out. He looked at the date and then waved us on.
>
> "Is that all right?" I asked.
>
> "Yes. Of course."
>
> We went up the street, past the whitewashed stone houses. . . .

The other passage is the climax of action of the novel, the bullfight:

> When he had finished his work with the muleta and was ready to kill, the crowd made him go on. They did not want the bull killed yet, they did not want it to be over. Romero went on. It was like a course in bull-fighting. All the passes he linked up, all completed, all slow, templed and smooth. There were no tricks and no mystifications. There was no brusqueness. And each pass as it reached the summit gave you a sudden ache inside. The crowd did not want it ever to be finished.
>
> The bull was squared on all four feet to be killed, and Romero killed directly below us. He killed not as he had been forced to by the last bull, but as he wanted to. He profiled directly in front of the bull, drew the sword out of the folds of the muleta and sighted along

the blade. The bull watched him. Romero spoke to the bull and tapped one of his feet. The bull charged and Romero waited for the charge, the muleta held low, sighting along the blade, his feet firm. Then without taking a step forward, he became one with the bull, the sword was in high between the shoulders, the bull had followed the low-slung flannel, that disappeared as Romero lurched clear to the left, and it was over. The bull tried to go forward, his legs commenced to settle, he swung from side to side, hesitated, then went down on his knees, and. . . . Handkerchiefs were waving all over the bull-ring. The President looked down from the box and waved his handkerchief. . . .

These passages are, of course, artfully different—within the narrow range of language that Hemingway uses. The short, active, declarative sentences of the description are increasingly connected by "and" in the action, accelerating the tempo; finally there are only commas, speed of speech. In the climactic sentence, "Then without taking a step etc.," the syntax is allowed to break down. The description has a natural randomness, as things turn up, including the pointless dialogue with the carabineer. In the action every sentence is pointed to the climax. In both passages, Hemingway uses the repetitions that are his favorite glue. But in the description they are more freely scattered and oddly equivocal in syntax: "road," "crossroads," "cross-straps," "crossed," "sides of the road," "side-streets"; "levelled down," "got down," "handed down." In the action, the repetitions follow more directly and are univocal, urgent, plangent: "they did not want," "they did not want it over," "he wanted to"; "killed," "killed," "killed"; "directly below us," "directly in front of the bull"; "charged," "waited for the charge"; "handkerchiefs were waving," "waved his handkerchief."

Nevertheless, the two passages have overwhelmingly in

common the chief characteristic of Hemingway's style, early and mature: The persons are held at arm's length, there is no way to get inside them or identify with them, it is happening to them. (But note that the events do not happen to the prose; rather the prose influences the events. For instance, it is because the driver handed *down* the bags and *ended* with the rod-case that the carabineer came *up* and pointed to the rod-case.)

In describing arriving in a new place, it is plausible that events happen to one; but in the passages of action it is almost uncanny—and this is why this is a remarkable style—how we still seem to hear: "it happened that the crowd did not want" or even "it happened to the crowd that it did not want"; "it happened to Romero that he wanted," "it happened that he profiled," "it happened to him that the bull charged," and "it happened that he met the charge." This has gotten to be the style of "objective" journalism, but it was writers like Hemingway who invented the style for the journalists. The verbs are active and the sentences indicative, but since the *persons* do not do it, we feel that they do not *do* it. And this is how the author has plotted it in the preceding pages anyway.

The narrator too is mesmerized by what he is telling. The effect is not at all like the impressionism of Virginia Woolf, for she lets us experience the first person knower, who grows. But as I have said, it is like the Brechtian "alienation," which Hemingway achieves more consistently than Brecht.[3]

That we exist in a meaningless universe—vanity of vanities—is the theme of *The Sun Also Rises,* with its motto and title taken from Ecclesiastes; and this novel,

3. In one of his aphorisms, Kafka says, "I have long since fallen under the wheels—comfortingly enough." But in his stories he persists in asking why; he feels insulted. Hemingway is baffled beyond insult.

though not powerful, is authentic through and through. In Hemingway's later works, the more romantic or adventurous themes are betrayed by the passive style. (*The Old Man and the Sea* has some authenticity, but the style is richer.) Ideally, the style of any work should be the style *of* that work, a unique language saying what the whole work wants to say. But of course, with Hemingway and most of us, our style is our way of being in the world in general rather than for just this one book. We are wise to choose our subjects according to what we *can* say. In the best cases, we choose on the borderline and learn to say more. Hemingway played it a little too safe.

To make my point, let me contrast this passive style with a powerful active style. I unfairly choose a very great passage. Here is the exordium of the opening section of *The Decline and Fall of the Roman Empire.*

For three long chapters Gibbon has been describing and (more or less) extolling the Roman Empire under the Antonines—its extent, its power, its prosperity, its arts, its institutions and civil peace, the occasional beneficence of its rulers. He concludes:

But the empire of the Romans filled the world, and, when that empire fell into the hands of a single person, the world became a safe and dreary prison for his enemies. The slave of Imperial despotism, whether he was condemned to drag his gilded chain in Rome and the senate, or to wear out a life of exile on the barren rock of Seriphus, or the frozen banks of the Danube, expected his fate in silent despair. To resist was fatal, and it was impossible to fly. On every side he was encompassed with a vast extent of sea and land, which he could never hope to traverse without being discovered, seized, and restored to his irritated master. Beyond the frontiers, his anxious view could discover nothing, except the ocean, inhospitable deserts, hostile tribes of barbarians, of fierce manners and unknown language, or dependent kings, who would gladly purchase the emperor's protection by the sacrifice of an obnoxious fugitive. "Wherever you are," said Cicero to the exiled Marcellus, "remember that you are equally within the power of the conqueror."

Whether in his enlightened awareness or in his Enlightenment prejudice, there is no doubt that Gibbon is in complete control of the vast scene and appropriates it for the reader. In each sentence he exhausts the alternative situations, the possibilities of action, the geographical space of the world. The ideas are many and not repeated, the motion is rapid for an elegant style, yet he gives us all the balances and parallels and even a chiasmus. Without losing speed, he builds to longer sentences, grander territory, bleaker scenery, and more desperate gloom. Yet, though he has the story in his grip, he is by no means cold or detached; he does not strangle himself. Nearly every sentence has something sarcastic or spiteful: "safe prison," "gilded chain in the senate," "irritated master," "obnoxious fugitive." He is not talking about an abstraction; we are made to identify with that hyperactive, and balked, victim. And the plotted place of this bitter outburst, after the (rather) golden narration that precedes, is like a blow.

Return now to Hemingway and his narrow range. It is not surprising that a succession of short active indicative sentences produces passivity. We turn to each verb after it has struck. There is not enough syntactical leeway for the author or reader to become engaged either actively or contemplatively or as one who desires or one who interprets. An advantage of the style is that it is in close contact with the facts being told, since there is no intermediary of indirect discourse, point of view, subordination, explanation. This is its aptness for journalistic reporting. A disadvantage is that it can rapidly become boring, as Hemingway often is, because it is hard to make the bits add up and there is increasing resistance to taking the bits in. When Hemingway is good, he provides glue—repetitions or leading tones like the rod-case.

But Hemingway certainly used the style also hoping to tell simple, down-to-earth experience, and in this crucial respect the style doesn't work, since it is not how we experience. In a previous chapter, I made the same point against taking short active indicative sentences as the syntactical kernels of all sentences. The empirical world that is told by them is not primary experience, and we see that when such sentences are actually spun out, the effect is human passivity.

We are again faced with the puzzle that we met in discussing the static style of the Egyptians according to Henri Frankfort. If Hemingway's style is so persistently passive in effect, how can it cope with enough of human life to be viable? I can think of four ways in which Hemingway countervails the passive effect of his prose.

First, obviously, is the violent *macho* activism of the characters and events he couches in the prose, nothing but bull-fighters, warriors, gun-packing gangsters, hunters of big animals and big fish. But this becomes real thin real soon. One begins to psychoanalyze it simply because there is nothing else to do with it. One wishes that the chosen sport was baseball, with teammates, or that he wrote about equally manly tasks like farming or carpentry, so that there could be some product more interesting than a corpse.

Second, he knows better. There is a unique sentence in *The Sun Also Rises* that is a most peculiar development of the accustomed style. The whole passage is a deviation. A man has been killed on the street by a bull being driven to the ring, and a waiter at the café comments that it's a stupid kind of fun and not for him. The narrator says,

> The bull who killed Vicente Girones was named Bocanegra, was Number 118 of the bull-breeding establishment of Sanchez Taberno, and was killed by Pedro Romero as the third bull of that same afternoon. His ear was cut by popular acclamation and given to Pedro Romero, who, in turn, gave it to Brett, who wrapped it in a handkerchief belonging to myself, and left both ear and handkerchief, along with a number of Muratti cigarette-stubs, shoved far back in the drawer of the bed-table that stood beside her bed in the Hotel Montoya, in Pamplona.

This unusually long and uncharacteristically complex sentence is the only spunky sentence in the book, and one of the few in Hemingway's work. It tells a rebellious, not passive, response: bitter contempt. Once the short active sentences are brought synoptically together, the effect is to write them off, to tell the world off. But though he *knows* this, Hemingway cannot follow it up, so that the passage is merely sentimental. (Sentimentality is feeling or "significance" more than the plot warrants.) Instead he goes on to the bull-fight and, as if on the rebound, to the one overwritten paragraph in the book, "Pedro Romero had the greatness. Etc.," which is hopelessly sentimental. Instead of taking his own rage as meaningful, he makes a desperate bid to find a hero, an agent. It doesn't wash.

The rejected theme reappears years later, however, as the rueful message of *The Old Man and the Sea,* that you try like the devil and bring back bones. The later book is not spunky, it rationalizes; but it is a hard look at himself.

(Incidentally, the bull's ear that Brett leaves behind with the cigarette butts, embarrassedly in the back of the drawer, is the real literary probability for her walking out on the young bull-fighter in the ending, and not the lofty renunciation that some of the critics seem to read. What *does* one do with shitty underwear or a bull's ear, in a hotel?)

A third way in which Hemingway countervails the passive hypothesis of his style is his stoical ethic. It appears not in the subject matter nor the prose, but in the plotting: The people are loyal, they endure, they go it alone. This ethic is surely why he was so popular and seemed to be a major writer during his era. He gave people something to live on with, when the conditions were so absurd. But he did not have enough intellect to assert a lasting ethical position. My impression is that young people today do not find him "existential" enough. I have heard them seriously ask what difference it would make if the human race vanished utterly. Hemingway would have been shocked by such an attitude, as I am. Put it this way: Normally, we would expect characters in novels, especially toward the end, to do something, influence events. In Hemingway's novels the characters are done to, but at least they *are* done to by the events, they are engaged in them. In many recent novels, however, the characters just "make the scene"; they are not engaged in the events but are like tourists. Or they con it like hipsters. They seem to have infinite time. Hemingway understood that people get worn out, grow old.

But yin and yang. In contemporary writing there wells up a flood of very personal reporting of actual political events in which the authors have taken part. More passionate and reflective than objective journalism, less plotted and universal than poetic fiction, this kind has become a new genre since it fills the need of the times. So far as I have read, Barbara Deming is the best. Norman Mailer is an interesting transitional writer. He is caught in an ethic partly Hemingway and partly hipster; he

gravitates to the new subject matter, but he is not committed to its actions and therefore becomes decorative.
(Reminds me of Carlyle.)

In my opinion, Hemingway's work will last not because
of his stoical ethic but because of something in his style.
It is sweetness. It appears more frequently in books later
than *The Sun Also Rises*, especially in *A Farewell to Arms*.
When it appears, the short sentences coalesce and flow,
and sing—sometimes melancholy, sometimes pastoral,
sometimes personally embarrassed in an adult, not an
adolescent, way. In the dialogues, he pays loving attention
to the spoken word. And the writing is meticulous; he is
sweetly devoted to writing well. Most everything else is
resigned, but here he makes an effort, and the effort
produces lovely moments. The young, since they read
poorly, do not dig that writing is his "existential" act. As
Spinoza would say it: For a writer, his writing is his intellect in action, his freedom, whereas the themes he is
stuck with, his confusion, his audience, are likely to be his
human bondage.

5 . The Manner of Imitation

Style, the writer's hypothesis of how the world is,
shades quickly into his general point-of-view-as-an-author,
as Kierkegaard called it: how he himself is in the world
when he says, how he relates his saying to what is said.
Does he identify himself with his subject matter as it un-
folds and speak directly for it? Does he maintain his own
difference and comment on the subject matter? Does he
perhaps disown the subject matter, hold it away, alienate
it? Is he plain, philosophical, ironic, humorous, paradoxical, sardonic?

In the *Poetics,* Aristotle has a rudimentary discussion of

how the poet takes the subject, which he calls the "manner of imitation," distinguishing it from the "means of imitation," which is speech, and from the "object of imitation," the actions of men better or worse than ordinary. He distinguishes two manners: In the dramatic manner, the poet vanishes himself and lets the actors speak directly and act him out; in the narrative manner, the poet maintains his own identity, talks about the action, and sometimes uses indirect discourse.

In modern times, however, the kind of involvement of the author has become almost the chief topic of esthetics. Starting from the distinction of tragedy and epic, Goethe and Schiller brilliantly posed it as a peculiarly modern issue: the difference between naive and self-conscious poetry. And now for two hundred years we have discussed Romanticism and Classicism, Realism and Naturalism, Symbolism, Impressionism and Cubism, the Revolution of the Word, Surrealism, and so forth. These are Manners. They imply differences in style—they are statements about the world; but even more, they are statements about the author's attitude toward writing and toward language.

(1) In principle, there are opposite ways of achieving the pure dramatic manner: either by vanishing the narrator into the actors, as in plays, or by making the action identical with the speech of the narrator, as in lyric poems said by "I." In fact, however, plays are rarely authentically dramatic. Except in real rituals in a community of faith—Artaud cites the trance-plays of Bali—the actors are ventriloquists' dummies; they do not speak for themselves. Euripides is not Medea; he is giving words to her and manipulating the plot. Shakespere is even less dramatic; he shifts the locale from scene to scene and contrasts the scenes, no different from Homer. The maxim that Aristotle

gives to playwrights—keep out of it, *"ars celare artem"*—is itself a proof of inauthenticity.

Indeed, the most authentically objective speech that we have—the speaker lost into the action—is the operational language of physical science, provided that the speaker is truly exploring nature and writing down her sentences as he goes. A scientist is not ironical nor humorous. It is what it is. (In fact, of course, most science proceeds on hypothetical preconceptions and is not dramatic.)

Lyric poets often approximate the dramatic manner by the opposite route, by transforming the action into the flow of their own words. We saw that Wordsworth sometimes hit it off by the action of his syntax. I agree with Poe that such lyric poems must be short, for once we have to hold the parts of a long discourse in memory, they must be arranged from outside and we have lost the pure dramatic manner. (Pound called Noh plays the only long lyric poems: By the contrast of poetry, music, dance, and silence, it is possible to construct a longer immediate experience.)

In all cases, the formal property of the dramatic manner is the unity of time and place. The plot of a play fills the time it takes to act it, without intermissions or changes of scene, which would be interventions of the narrator.[4] A scientific demonstration is just the statement of the operations required for its conclusion, without hypothesis or interpretation. A lyric poem is the arc of its feeling; it rather quickly climaxes and fades.

(2) Once we have gotten beyond primitive plays and

4. Aristotle's rule for the unity of time, "to keep as far as possible within a single circuit of the sun," is not so unphilosophical as it seems. Just as in painting, foreshortened perspective or Chinese perspective looks more "real" than mathematical perspective, so the hurried telescoping of a day's events seems like the "actual" time that a tragic or comic plot occupies. By contrast, Coleridge complains that *Othello* is unpleasantly dragged out in time for the kind of play it is.

ballads, however, or the simplest observation of nature and craftsmanship, most writing is self-conscious: The author maintains his identity and says *his* say, intervening, commenting, hypothesizing, ironizing. A playwright gives the actors words to say. A novelist not only manipulates the story but sometimes says his own thoughts in his own person. In Pindar's long poems, it is the posture that Pindar strikes that gives structure and interest to his inevitably monotonous subject matter. Unless he is an anatomist or a simon-pure naturalist, a scientist cannot simply let nature speak; he makes an experiment rather than a demonstration; he is testing his own hypothesis. An historian, who is not a mere chronicler, selects and arranges. As a social critic, I have my own ideas of what is good for the Americans, and I describe our present institutions accordingly.

The formal property of all narratives is that there are two plots interacting: the narrated action in the third person and the narrator's plot, either spoken or constructible, in the first person. There is the description and the system of hypotheses, the story and the commentary. The allegory has a moral, and conversely, the feeling of the poet has an "objective correlative" in the imagery of the poem. Art, the process of literature, is to make a whole that is *resistant* to analysis into these parts. Otherwise, the effect is trivial. An explicit allegory is frigid. A scientific statement that is merely illustrated by an "experiment" is a lecture, not science. Social criticism must be more than applied ideology for political purposes. A story is not an essay, and an essay is not an autobiography.

It is good advice for a young poet to write prose essays, so he can get rid of his ideas. As a veteran writer, I like to flirt with saying objective ideas as personally as I can. Artistically, the narrator and the subject matter are a dialogue—and since the world is not at risk, it must be the narrator who takes the risk.

The narrative manner is the *grandeur et misère* of the intellect. Because authors stand firm and will not surrender their identity, we are of some use. We refuse to be stupider than we are. But because we have to mess with the subject matter of the world—it is all the subject matter that there is—we cannot say *our* say.

But God, Milton tells us, does not speak in indirect discourse. Here is a linguistic analysis from *Tetrachordon*. The issue is that Malachi, ii,16, can bear alternative translations, either "I hateth putting away, saith the Lord God" or "The Lord God saith he hateth putting away." Milton calls attention to the difference of manner and decides,

> Reject the second reading, because it introduces in a new manner the person of God speaking less majestic than He is ever wont. When God speaks by His prophet, he never speaks in the prophet's first person. He would have said, "I hate putting away," said the Lord, and not send word by Malachi in a sudden fallen style, shrinking the glorious omnipotence of God speaking into a kind of circumscriptive absence. As if a herald in the achievement of a king should set his helmet sideways and close, not full-faced and open in the posture of direction and command.

(3) Besides the dramatic manner in which the author identifies with the action, and the narrative manner in which he entertains it, there is a third possibility: to disown the subject matter, to hold it away as something that he is not willing to mean. I don't think the ancients thought of this; they took meaningful language for granted. But now the alienating manner is becoming fairly prevalent.

Brecht proposed holding the play away by making it into an object and attaching labels to it. We have seen that some refuse literature altogether, as irrelevant, and some distrust language itself, as a trap.

When scientists formulate their sentences as part of the System of Science rather than as exploring the unknown, they disown nature and come on as obsessional priests of an idol. Value-neutral social science states the repudiation of literature as an explicit principle. The next step is to fill the void of meaning by multiplying the methodology:

> The more horses you yoke, the quicker everything goes—not the rending of the block from its foundation, which is impossible, but the snapping of the traces and with that the gay and empty journey. [Kafka]

More honorable is the icy withdrawal of the author in literary Naturalism, which also says the social facts without evaluation or comment. But it is a rebellious statement: "*There* is the world—damn it!" The author vanishes himself in order to have no part of it. When—and if—he reappears, it is to speak in unintelligible tongues, as at Pentecost.

6 . Does Literature Progress?

Naturally, most writers in most periods are not inventive stylists but write the style that is currently standard, a mix of traditional elements. Good style does not need to be novel, but it must be genuine, coming from how the writer is, speaking his animal cries, squaring with what he sees, not avoiding the others, not censoring. It is his colloquial speech, but more artful. And since the common style of any going culture is always a viable hypothesis, it might be a writer's own, with little new in it. To offer an analogy, we put a pot of water on the stove and light a fire and boil the water. This is not the kind of experiment that is printed up in *Science* or *Nature,* but it is excellent natural science—controlled, replicable, and predictive.

On this analogy, we might say, though not exactly, that there is progress in literature and the other fine arts as there is in natural science. Just as exceptional investigators go from boiling water to the theory of the motion of molecules and to thermodynamics, so there are refinements of a standard literary style leading to quite new developments; a simple factual letter leads to Richardson's epistolary novels, to Balzac's realism, to Flaubert's naturalism, Mallarmé's naturalism, and Joyce's naturalism. It is usually denied that arts and letters progress in this sense, for we do not now have actual writing occurring with the *accumulated* power of Sophocles, Milton, and Tolstoy, whereas in science, even if Archimedes, Newton, and Einstein are dead, contemporary scientists have the power of their science. (I think this objection is valid, and we must ask why it is so.) Yet a reasonably learned writer does have resources of style from a long tradition, and he has access to once unknown or forbidden subject matter won for him by the personal suffering, moral courage, and often physical courage of previous writers. Even in one generation, in 1970 I write and freely publish what in 1940 I used to write with the chill of not being able to publish.

But an analogy with physical sciences is inexact for several reasons. First, literature is more like psychology and the social sciences in that, over the centuries, there is really not much added empirical information or observation to build on progressively. Aristotle had nearly as much empirical experience in the social sciences as we do. The Greeks talked, behaved and introspected, reared children, did business, used political persuasion, made war, exploited, exercised authority, and tried to administer justice, as much as we do. There have been no new mechanical instruments yielding spectacular new information, like telescopes, spectroscopes, and microscopes. New methods, like free association or questionnaires, have pretty good ancient analogues. The most important real advance has been better census-taking. (I am not impressed by the yield of mere method, like computer simulation or content analysis.)

Again, in the social sciences (and literature) the data do not accumulate also for the opposite reason: Too much is always too different. Social facts are rarely isolable and controllable. There are few crucial experiments. Behavior is concrete and complex. With any important historical change, there are radically new set-ups. So a wise investigator is satisfied to make sense of the concrete situation that confronts him, without trying for abstract generalization, quantitative precision, and accounting for all the phenomena. He certainly is chary of predicting. There is a certain amount of development as we adjust old formulas, e.g. Marxism, to changed situations that they do not quite fit, but there is hardly a spectacular forward march. Incidentally, in my opinion there has been far more progress in arts and letters than in the social sciences; at least they have not been so ideological and self-destructively polemical. We can admire and learn from a poem even when it does not do our thing.

Fine arts and letters are even more densely concrete than social sciences. As we noticed in discussing the literary process, a writer's biographical memory and personal needs are among the essentials he works with. Thus, in a sense, each work *is* a crucial experiment of its style and the author's personality, and this is an advantage over the social sciences, which have hardly any crucial experiments. This is why artworks usually have life, while social science is usually lifeless. (The remedy is to make social science frankly political, experimental—politics has plenty of life.)

Finally, all high creation, in art *or* natural science, is

committed and passional, risks oneself, goes out on a limb. But in a special science, although the act of the scientist is personal, it is easier to add onto other people's work, because the problems tend to be common and the method is definite. In a fine art the problem itself is so individuated that the solution seems sometimes to be a brand new beginning, though it never really is. In sciences, routine performance adds its bit to what has been achieved, but in arts and letters, routine performance, that does not risk enough of the author's soul, is peculiarly lifeless. A talented music student can turn out a creditable "Haydn" symphony, but there is no point to it; what it lacks is the need to write that way that Haydn had. It requires enormous power to rework Homer, as Virgil and Milton did; most imitators do not have enough of their own to carry it off; most powerful writers have other things to do. Yet we must not overestimate the need for idiosyncratic genius. Rather, authenticity. Horace says that a poem is great or it is nothing, but he goes too far. If a work is honest, original in the sense of being one's own, it improves the culture, makes better readers for a better writer. This is a cumulative effect.

There is an inevitable illusion of historical perception that occurs in contrasting literature and science. Since literary works are so desperately personal, subsequent readers identify with them. Human beings are both sunk in history and plastic to make themselves anew, including imitating history; so they manage to make poets of the past relevant to themselves by some handle or other. But individual achievements in objective science are by-passed and absorbed into the system of science. We notice that there is no Milton alive, not only because we do not do as well but because Milton is still with some of us. But Galileo is only a figure of the history of science; a scientist might use his findings and never know his name. So the progress of science to the present as a *system* is self-evident, whereas arts and letters seem to consist of scattered great names, mostly of dead persons.

To sum up. We cannot expect literature to have the molecular progress of science; it is more jumpy by nature. Yet there is a kind of systematic progress of available styles and subject matters. In a normal civilized period this tradition is the source of the standard style that most writers use—journalists, scholars in all fields, popular essayists and popular novelists. Occasionally, by an act of inventive genius, a standard style is newly consolidated, for instance Dryden's English. Then it is quite evident that all the writers are benefiting from an accumulated past.

CHAPTER XI

Format and "Communications"

1. Format and Empty Speech

By "format" I mean imposing on the literary process a style that is extrinsic to it. The dictionary tells the history very well:

> **Format.** —*n.* 1. the shape and size of a book as determined by the number of times the original sheet has been folded to form the leaves. 2. the general physical appearance of a book, magazine, or newspaper, such as the type face, binding, quality of paper, margins, etc. 3. the organization, plan, style, or type of something: *They tailored their script to a half-hour format. The format of the show allowed for topical and controversial gags.* 4. *Computer Technol.* the organization or disposition of symbols on a magnetic tape, punch card, or the like, in accordance with the input requirements of a computer, card-sort machine, etc. —*v.t.* 5. *Computer Technol.* to adapt (the organization or disposition of coded

information) on a magnetic tape, punch card, or the like, to conform to the input requirements of a computer, card-sort machine, etc.

Format has no literary power, and finally it destroys literary power. It is especially disastrous to the common standard style, because it co-opts it and takes the heart out of it.

Thus, an editor chops a sentence here and there, and also my last paragraph, because 3,000 words is the right length for the format of his magazine. An assistant editor rewrites me just to be busy and earn his keep. A daily column must appear though the columnist has nothing to say that day. An editor of *Harper's* asks me to simplify an argument because, he says, the readers of the magazine cannot digest more than two thoughts to one article. At another magazine they rewrite in Time-style. A young fellow writes his thesis in the style of professional competence of his department. Obviously, the effect of format is worse if the writer must adapt himself and write, rather than just having his writing mashed. Since writing is inherently spontaneous and original, a writer cannot produce what is not his own without a broken spirit.

American television is especially productive of format. The networks are a big investment of capital, so broadcasting time is cut up for sale to the fraction of a minute, and programs are tailored to the strips. A mass medium aims at a big audience, so the programs must be sensational enough to attract many and bland enough not to offend any. In the peculiar system of semi-monopolies, where a few baronial firms compete in such a way as to keep one another in business, if one network hits on a new show or newscast, the others at once program a close imitation. Legally the channels are public property, so the licensed stations must be politically impartial and present all sides of controversial issues; the most convenient way of handling this is to present no controversial issue. But there is another rule that a certain fraction of time must be devoted to public service, including political controversy; and a way of economically handling this is to have a panel of wildly divergent points of view debating an issue for the required twenty-six minutes. This sometimes produces heat, never light, usually nothing. It is a format. What is glaring in the whole enterprise is the almost entire lack of will to *say* anything, rather than just provide a frame for the ads.[1]

Format is not like censorship that tries to obliterate speech, and so sometimes empowers it by making it important. And it is not like propaganda that simply tells lies. Rather, authority imposes format on speech because it needs speech, but not autonomous speech. Format is speech colonized, broken-spirited. It is a use of speech as social-cement, but it is not like the small talk of acquaintances on the street in their spontaneous style; it is a collective style for a mass. So in appearance it is often indistinguishable from the current literary standard. But in actual use it is evident from the first sentence that it does not tell anything.

Of course, empty style is nothing new. Diplomats, administrators of all kinds, and other public relators, who have to make remarks about what is none of our business, have always used a style to drain meaning from what they say. It can be a fine art—cf. Proust on the virtuosity of Norpois. But modern society has unique resources of technology and social organization to separate speech from living speakers. I do not think that any previous era has ever worked up a universal pedagogy and a general Theory

1. In my fallible memory, the ads themselves used to have a more authentic style—more cinematic, more musical, even more poetical—because they had a real rhetorical purpose, to sell goods. But my recent observation is that they too have become lifeless. Is this because of the imposition of new extrinsic regulations, e.g. not to lie, not to sell carcinogens or dangerous toys, not to increase air pollution, etc.? It is hard to be a frank huckster anymore.

of Communications to sidetrack human speech as such. In Newspeak, George Orwell was shooting at not quite the right target. He was thinking of *control* of speech by the lies and propaganda of crude totalitarian regimes; but I doubt that this is humanly feasible. (In the end the State is bound together by simple fright, not brainwashing.) The government of a complicated modern society cannot lie *much*. But by format, even without trying, it can kill feeling, memory, learning, observation, imagination, logic, grammar, or any other faculty of free writing.

2

The schools try hard to teach the empty style. There is frantic anxiety about the schools' failing to teach children to read and write; there have been riots on the street about it; the President of the United States has called the matter our top priority. But so far as I know, none of those who are frantic—parents rich and poor, nor the President— have pointed out that reading and writing spring from speaking, our human way of being in the world; that they are not tools but arts, and their content is imagination and truth. Occasionally a sensitive teacher pipes up that children might learn reading and writing if these were interesting and sprang from what the children wanted to know and had to say, if they were relevant to their personal lives and had some practical function. But mostly the remedies that are proposed are mechanical or administrative; there are debates between sounding out and word recognition and quarrels about who controls the schools.

The reason for anxiety is simply that if children do not learn the tools of reading and writing, they cannot advance through school, and if they don't get school diplomas, they won't get well-paying jobs in a mandarin society. Literacy is incidental, a kind of catalyst that drops out of the equation. To pass the tests really requires just the same verbal skills—nothing much else has been learned—and there is no correlation between having the diplomas and competence in any job or profession. School style exists for the schools. So some of us have suggested that if it and they did not exist, that too would be very well. (Rather, change the rules for licensing and hiring.)

In most urban and suburban communities, most children will pick up the printed code anyway, school or no school. (In ghetto and depressed rural communities, they might not.) It is likely that schoolteaching destroys more genuine literacy than it produces. But it is hard to know if most people think that reading and writing have any value anyway, either in themselves or for their use, except that they are indispensable in how we go about things. Contrast the common respect for mathematics, which are taken to be *about* something and are powerful, productive, magical; yet there is no panic if people are mathematically illiterate.

Thus, during the long years of compulsory schooling, reading and writing are a kind of format, an imposed style with no intrinsic relation to good speech. And this must be characteristic of any mandarin society, even when, as in medieval China, the style of literacy happens to be the standard literary classics. With us, as school reading and writing cease to have literary meaning, university study of Literature ceases to be about human speech, speech in its great examples. (It is a nice question, what university English studies *are* about.) And as fewer people read authentically, on-going literature may well become one of the minor arts, for connoisseurs, like rose gardening or weaving.

Naturally, when the imposing authority takes itself seriously as right and good, as in the Soviet Union, mandarin literacy is affirmed as excellent, the vehicle of all social and scientific progress, as well as the way to get ahead. Consider the following of the Russian pedagogue L. S. Vygotsky, which seems to say that it is necessary to *destroy* natural style:

> In learning to write, the child must disengage himself from the sensory aspect of speech and replace words by images of words. It is the abstract quality of language that is the main stumbling block to learning to write, not the underdevelopment of small muscles. . . . Our studies show that a child has little motivation to learn writing when we begin to teach it. Written language demands conscious work. . . . The concrete totality of traits [must be] destroyed through abstraction; then the possibility of unifying traits on a different basis opens up. Only the mastery of abstraction enables the child to progress to the formation of genuine concepts.

This odd view of writing and teaching writing is the precise opposite of a literary approach, e.g. Sylvia Ashton-Warner's, which tries to get writing from the child's spontaneous native speech, with all its sensuality and animal need. (We shall see later that by "genuine concepts" Vygotsky means the social ideology.)[2]

The use of words is already detachment from, control of, the stream of experience; to go the further step of Vygotsky is to control the speaker. It is a socially-induced aphasia.

2. It is astonishing that Vygotsky can believe what he says. In another passage he shrewdly and accurately points out how the school set-up predetermines the child's responses: "Piaget's findings are valid only for his special kindergarten play milieu [encouraging] extensive soliloquizing. Stern points out that in a German kindergarten, where there is more group activity, the coefficient of egocentrism was somewhat lower. . . . The difference with Soviet children must be even greater." Indeed, in *all* cases a child must cope with the conditions that they impose on him, and re-adjust in order to survive. To do *this* is the child's nature.

In any case, the literature that is the fruit of this method of teaching writing is also taken very seriously, as the mandarin literacy is. It is carefully regulated in style, and it is reproduced in millions of copies. In Russia, writing that is more literary in a traditional sense does *not* become a minor art for connoisseurs, but is circulated in manuscript for a band of criminal conspirators.

3 . The Resistance of Colloquial Speech

The forces of format, "to conform to the input requirements" of a social or technical system, can quickly debase public language and the standard literary style. Strong writers are less affected; society does not know how to produce them and it does not even know how to inhibit them, except by violence.

But colloquial speech is quite impervious to corruption by format. It has an irrepressible vitality to defy, ridicule, or appropriate. It gobbles up format like everything else. There are too many immediate occasions, face-to-face meetings, eye-witnessings, common sense problems, for common speech to be regimented. People who can talk can be oppressed but not brainwashed. Modern cities are depressing and unhealthy, but the people are not mechanical.

Once out of bounds, children do not talk like school. In America, adults talk like school less than they used, because (I like to think) the school style has so little literary value that it's not worth adopting. Children imitate the TV, but soon do it sarcastically. Adults imitate the ads less than they used because there has been overexposure. The young are in revolt against the ads, so the ads lamely have to imitate the young. In totalitarian countries, even after a generation of benevolent instruction by all the schools, mass media, labor unions, etc., young Czechs and Poles, who have never known any other dispensation, have not learned what is good for them; apparently, they get their ideas by conversation with one another. American voters almost never repeat the sentences of politicians; rather, they tell you their own lay political theories and that they can't stand the personalities of certain candidates.

By and large, adolescents are the most susceptible to empty format. They often seem to take TV images for reality. In serious moments they often sound like a textbook in social psychology: A girl has a "meaningful relationship with her boy friend," people are "consumed by negative feelings toward someone in the group"—I am quoting from *WIN,* the best of the youth movement magazines. And it is amazing how the language of underground newspapers, identical by dozens, is actually spoken by teen-agers. But this language is less format than it seems. It is filling the vacuum of adolescent speechlessness. The stereotypes serve as glue for ganging together, and the ganging is real though the language is spurious. A rock festival is usually a commercial hoax, but the pilgrimage to it is not.

More poignant is the speech of a highly articulate, but unread, militant *chicano* housewife, who declaims social-worker Newspeak during a demonstration because she has no other public words. But her passion gives it life, if not sense.

The deep pathos of colloquial speech—with its indestructible good sense, eye-witnessing, communal vitality, and crotchetiness (including much private error and deep-rooted tribal prejudice)—is that in highly organized societies its field of operation is strictly limited. We can speak good colloquial where we have freedom to initiate and decide. When our actions are predetermined by institutional and political frameworks that are imposed on us, we necessarily become anxious, inconfident of ourselves, and we fall into institutional and ideological format and its mesmerized thoughts. Thus in our societies there is continually spoken a dual language: Intimately, people talk sense—about politics, the commodities, the schools, the police, etc.—yet they also talk format, and act on it. In totalitarian societies, where a strong effort is made to reform colloquial speech to official format, the effort cannot succeed, but people do begin to whisper and fall silent; finally, only a few brave writers, who have a very special obligation to honorable speech, continue to talk like human beings.[3]

In America, our colloquial is certainly not much improved by respectable literary models. It is a loss, because people would express themselves more clearly and forcefully if they could express themselves a little more literarily yet without sounding like a book, and they could thereby also extend the boundaries of their human expression into more public domains—at least somewhat (there would be conflict). A few of us writers do the best we can. Some of the young pick up our language—and turn it into *their* format!

3. Fortunately, there is hard evidence for my conjecture that modern people aren't "dehumanized." The Princeton Theological Seminary ran an ingenious experiment that showed that students stopped to help a (planted) man in need or passed him by not because of their gentleness or hardness of heart, but because they were told they had time or were late for an examination. Frederic Darley and Gregory Bateson suggest that the Good Samaritan of the parable was probably in a "low hurry" condition, while the priest and Levite were doubtlessly rushing: "One can imagine the priest and Levite, prominent public figures, hurrying along with little black books full of meetings and appointments, glancing furtively at their sun dials as they go. In contrast, the Samaritan, a man of much lower public status, would likely have fewer and less important people counting on him to be at a set place at a set time."

There *is* a kind of style to our speech. It is the style of urban confusion: a Yiddish that chews up and can assimilate the ads, the sociological jargon, the political double-talk, the canned entertainment.

To achieve the controlled and accurate transmission of messages, it is necessary finally to dispense with human speakers altogether, and let us now turn our attention to this.

4 . "Communications"

The primary idea of the art of communications is to open channels or provide technical means by which speakers can talk to one another, like couriers or telegraph or telephone. As the general Theory of Communications has developed, however—it is a new branch of philosophy —the idea has come to be to make the signals precise and perfectly transmissible by explaining away the speakers. I will briefly trace the steps of this curious outcome, quoting from some of the chief authors.

Most simply, and innocently, whenever we use any medium or technical means to convey our meaning, there must be some adjustment of the form of the message to be handled by the medium or the technology. An engineer of the telephone company who wants to improve reception of the signals will urge speakers to say the phonemes sharply, and he might suggest new pronunciations for very frequent words: "faiəv" for "five," "naiən" for "nine." The speakers must not speak too quick, too slow, too loud, too soft. In the fine arts, of course, the adaptation to the medium is what the whole art is about: The "object of imitation" must assume an entirely new form and live and breathe in the medium. From this beginning, the theorists at once take a giant step.

Words [says Julian Huxley]

are tools for dealing more efficiently with the business of existence; so that language is properly speaking a branch of technology.

Here the words are not adapted to the technology, they are themselves the technology. In this formulation, speaking is not to be considered as itself one of the free human actions—it is a means to expedite other actions. (One wonders what they are.) The study of language is suddenly no longer one of the humanities.

Regarding language as a technology, we can begin to refine what 'it must be.

> The communications engineer [says Roman Jakobson in a passage we have already noted]
> most properly approaches the essence of the speech event when he assumes that the optimal speaker and listener have at their disposal more or less the same "filing cabinet of prefabricated representations"; the addressor selects one of these preconceived possibilities and the addressee is supposed to make an identical choice from the same assembly of possibilities already foreseen and provided for.

Needless to say, this is a very different doctrine from what I have been calling either the literary process or colloquial speech, where the speaker, drawing on many powers and expressing his needs, modifies the language to fit the unique situation. But if speakers cannot creatively adjust to the conversation they are having, Jakobson's requirement is certainly a technological necessity for accurate transmission. Otherwise there will be guessing and sometimes not grasping what is meant at all, as if it were a foreign language.

It is in this sense that we must understand Jakobson's remark that

> The efficiency of a speech event demands the use of a common code by the participants.

The common code is not what the speakers have as a convenience, as they might have other common possessions; it is what they have as a law, that they must not tamper with. We have commented on many passages of Saussure and the cultural anthropologists, how this code is constant, supra-individualistic, and generalized. In the extreme view of Whorf, it predetermines what the speakers must think.

But next, according to Count Korzybski, we can make a more precise specification for the prefabricated representations that fill the filing cabinets and are the common code. They are, says the Count, the names of "facts" organized into classes and classes of classes, in levels of abstraction. Using abstractions

> integrates the cortico-thalamic functions [by] inducing an automatic delay of reactions which automatically stimulates the cortical region and regulates and protects the usually over-stimulated thalamic region.

On this theory, the use of right speech would preclude any forceful action or final satisfaction of life, for these always have concrete objects and become spontaneous. He seems to be describing what I call "acting in a chronic low-grade emergency"—cf. *Gestalt Therapy* (II, iii, 9, and II, xi, 4). But he tells us,

> The socio-cultural developments of civilization depend on the capacity to produce higher and higher abstractions.

Freud called this *Civilization and Its Discontents*.

For the pedagogy to teach this common code of higher abstractions, we return to L. S. Vygotsky:

> We define "consciousness" to denote awareness of the activity of the mind, the consciousness of being conscious. . . . A concept can become subject to consciousness and deliberate control only when it is part of a system. If consciousness means generalizing, generalization in turn means the formation of a superordinate

concept that includes the concept as a case. A super-ordinate concept implies the existence of a series of subordinates and a hierarchy. Thus the concept is placed within a system of relationships of generality. . . . In the scientific concepts that the child acquires in school, the relationship to an object is mediated from the start by some other concept. It is our contention that the rudiments of systematization first enter the child's mind by way of his contact with scientific concepts of the [teacher] and are then transferred to everyday concepts, changing their psychological structure from the top down. This is why certain thoughts cannot be communicated to children, even if they are familiar with the necessary words.[4]

Here at last is a prescription for transforming common speech itself into format. Just browbeat the child with verbal explanations that he cannot understand. Vygotsky spells it out in a remarkable example:

A child cannot use "because" in real life situations, but he can correctly finish sentences on social science subjects, e.g. "Planned economy is possible in the Soviet Union because there is no private property—all lands, factories, and plants belong to the workers and peasants." Why is he capable of performing the operation in this case? Because the teacher, working with the pupil, has explained, supplied information, questioned, corrected, and made the pupil explain. Later, in finishing the sentence about his bicycle, he makes use of the fruits of that collaboration, this time independently. . . . With the progressive isolation of speech for oneself, vocalization becomes unnecessary, and because of its growing structural peculiarities also impossible. In

4. It is interesting, but not surprising, that Kropotkin, who was an anarchist, makes exactly the contrary point: You can teach anything to a child or an unlearned peasant *if you yourself* understand it concretely and therefore can follow *his* understanding and offer it by the right handle.

reality, however, behind the symptoms of dissolution [of common speech] lies a progressive development, the birth of a new speech form.

This new speech is mandarin or format. Orwell was not thinking of anything nearly so sophisticated, in describing Newspeak. The trick of breaking the free spirit that is inherent in speaking is "to make the pupil explain." The way of breaking the spirit of a writer is to pay him to write what makes no sense to him in a style that is not his own.

I have quoted at length from the Russian savant partly for his dogged manner but especially because he adequately brings us to another great leap in the Theory of Communications—the elimination of speakers because they are supernumeraries. Since we have nullified the free action of speakers, their realm of choice, their individuality, their thalamic emotions, and their concrete experience, and since their thoughts are internalizations of top-down instruction in a system of generalizations, it is possible to lop them off with Ockham's razor and to say that communication is the transaction of the system of general signs. This is what Sir Julian Huxley does:

> Language provides a new environment for life to inhabit. I shall call it the Noösphere, after Teilhard de Chardin. As fish swim in the sea and birds fly in the air, so we think and feel our way through this collective mental world.

The Noösphere, in Teilhard, is the network of signals which has evolved to brood over the world like the program of a universal computer—the Abbé identifies it with Jesus.

(It is remarkable how, pushed to the extreme, the technological approach to language converges so exactly, in content and rhetoric, with the anti-technological humanism of the phenomenologists, pushed to the extreme; cf. Merleau-

Ponty's "Speech is like an *être,* like a universe. It is never limited except by further language." In the end, it makes little difference if the "collective mental world" is man's new environment, or a project of freedom, or, as with Vygotsky, the internalized ideology of the State. But none of these describes what it is like to speak a language.)

It remains only for the physical world, too, to become Communications, and this step is taken by Norbert Wiener, with the synoptic elegance of a mathematician. The form or pattern of matter, the ordering of entropy (= disorder), is information; to cause such patterns is communication:

> When I control the actions of another person, I communicate a message to him, although the message is in the imperative mood. . . . The commands through which we exercise control over our environment are a kind of information which we impart to it. . . . Information is a name for the content of what is exchanged with the outer world as we adjust to it and make our adjustment felt upon it.

Putting it this way, moreover, we could say that a bat communicates with the ball it hits; there is no reason to take the point of view that "we," human beings, are the communicators; there is nothing essential to the metaphor "inner" and "outer." Indeed, a human being may well be the *message:*

> The organism is seen as a message. Organism is opposed to chaos, to disintegration, to death, as message is to noise. To describe an organism we answer certain questions about it which reveal its pattern. It is the pattern maintained by homeostasis which is the touchstone of our personal identity—and this may be transmitted as a message, e.g. by wire. [To be sure,] any scanning of the human organism must be a probe going through all its parts, and will accordingly tend to de-

stroy the tissue on its way. To hold an organism stable while part of it is being slowly destroyed, with the intention of creating it out of other material elsewhere . . . in most cases would destroy life. In other words, the fact that we cannot telegraph the pattern of a man seems to be due to technical difficulties—the idea itself is highly plausible.

Wiener does not envisage the man as a respondent or speaker who might interpret what is going on or object to it, for instance by saying "Ouch!" If he would say "Ouch!" however, would not this continually interject new information and put the scanner always one step behind? [5]

Thus, I have brought together half a dozen passages by important authors to show the kind of thing that sets my teeth on edge in modern theory of language. But I am sorry to conclude with a passage from Norbert Wiener, a real humanist who usually made a lot of sense and whom I have liked to quote on *my* side.

5 . *Avant Garde*

The deliberate response to format is *avant garde*— writing which devotes itself, at least in part, to flouting the standard style, to offending the audience. *Avant garde* is different from other inventive writing. If a work is felt to

5. In his idea of sending the pattern of the man by wire and re-creating him out of other material, Wiener holds the ancient doctrine of Prime Matter—a position somewhat like that of Santayana, with his Realm of Essence and Realm of Matter. It is not a tenable doctrine. As Aristotle pointed out, "Only the flute has the song of the flute": In actuality, form is the form of its own matter, and we know matter only as the potentiality of that form. I am pretty sure that a man is not given by his homeostasis. Conversely, the matter that makes up that homeostasis, not to speak of the man, is not just any "other material elsewhere," but is highly pre-formed and might be the devil to collect.

be "experimental," it is not that the writer is doing something new but that he is making an effort to be different, to be not traditional.

In any period, powerful artists are likely to go way out and become incomprehensible. They abide by the artistic imperative to make it as clear as possible, but they are not deterred by the fact that the audience doesn't catch on. They do not want to shock the audience, but the audience just gets lost—and bored. Thayer comments on the first performance of *Eroica:*

> Some, Beethoven's particular friends, assert that it is just this symphony which is his masterpiece, that this is the true style for high class music, and that if it does not please, it is because the public is not cultured enough artistically to grasp all these lofty beauties. After a few thousand years have passed, it will not fail of its effect. . . . A man shouted down from the gallery, "I'll give another kreutzer if the thing will but stop!"

Yet pretty soon, it made itself an audience, it taught people to speak, as Merleau-Ponty puts it well. On hindsight, the incomprehensible of genius almost always turns out to be in the mainstream of tradition, because the artist took the current style for granted, he worked on the boundary of what he knew, and he did something just more than he knew.

Avant garde artists do not take the current style for granted; it disgusts them. They do not care about the present audience; they want to upset it. Instead of trying to be as clear as possible, they are just as pleased to be incomprehensible, *fumiste* or *blagueur.* A sign of success, or success itself, could be to provoke a riot.[6]

6. But audiences are unpredictable. Sometimes—as at the premieres of *Ernani* and *Le Sacre du Printemps*—they are terribly sensitive in their philistinism and riot at works that were certainly not meant to offend. On the other hand, when recently my friends

Of course, such a disruptive attitude does not foster beautiful and finished works "exemplary to future generations" (Kant); the writer is too busy with making an effect to give himself to the literary process. *Avant garde* tends to be capricious, impatient, fragmentary, ill-tempered. Yet, except by raging and denying, a writer might not be able to stay alive at all as a writer. As a style, *avant garde* is an hypothesis that something is very wrong in society. The icy objectivity of the Naturalism of the turn of the century said that people were hypocrites. The Revolution of the Word said that the values of the civilization that fought the First World War were not acceptable; one could not talk "their" way. Surrealism said that rationality was a sell. As the century has worn on and wears on, these startling literary guesses have gotten a certain amount of confirmation.

An ultimate step is always Dada, the use of art to deny the existence of meaning. A step after the last is to puff up examples of format itself to giant size, Pop.

But in a confused society, *avant garde* does not flourish very well. What is done in order to be idiotic can easily be co-opted as the idiotic standard.

Some artists use the cast-off debris of technological society as their raw material. My brother goes in for decorating styrofoam packaging. It is just the opposite of the dadaist impulse to paint a mustache on "Mona Lisa."

A different direction altogether is to deny that literature as such is relevant—to say that writing is made honest only by its workaday and community use. In its philosophical form, which I remember hearing during the Twenties (e.g. *Gebrauchsmusik*), this is a profound doctrine. It is close to Goethe's great sentence that "Occasional poetry is

---

of the Living Theater tried to get their goats with a determined *avant garde* happening, the New York intellectuals just sat there and enjoyed every boring minute.

the highest kind"—the poetry of weddings, parties, funerals, and dedications. Street theater and commedia dell'arte are the utopia of every playwright. Music and plastic art—though literature less—have certainly flourished in service to religion. It is a doctrine of happy communities.

Since the Thirties, however, and very much nowadays, the irrelevance of literature has gotten to mean that the right use of literary speech is political action, like protest songs and guerilla theater; we simply don't have the community necessary for celebration, occasional poetry, and commedia dell'arte. That is, the process of literature is not used in its natural power to find meaning and make sense, so that we can act in a world that has meaning and sense. It is claimed there is no time for this; there is too much suffering and injustice. And only by engaging in revolutionary action can one produce new thought and lively words. But in practice, I have found, this comes to not questioning slogans that are convenient for an immediate tactic or a transient alliance. The writers tell half-truths. "Action" becomes idiotic activism. The vocabulary and grammar are pitched to a condescending populism, about at the level of junior high school, including the dirty words. The thought is ideological through and through. By a "revolutionary" route we come right back to format.

6. What Is Communication?

A more interesting dissent is the distrust of language as a means of human communication. If speech has become an exchange between filing cabinets of prefabricated representations, to speak is to be oneself a cog in the International Business Machine. Verbal arguments are nothing but Ping-Pong games that tap the ball back and

forth and avoid contact. Or they are ego trips to put one
another down and confirm one's own conceited self-image.
For people to know one another, it is better to touch, hold
hands, make love, or manhandle. The only trustworthy
words are emotional cries. These are the techniques of
sensitivity training and group psychotherapy. Some believe that under the influences of the right drugs they share
their thoughts and feelings. There is a revival of silent
meditation.

This is the outcome of regarding language as essentially a constant code, not to be modified by its speakers,
when people become alienated from all the institutions,
including language. Long schooling increasingly attempts
to socialize to the common code. Suburban life and mass
consumption of mass-produced commodities extend the
socialization into every detail of life. Communications
engineers tailor speech to make transactions more efficient.
Linguists devise ingenious formulas for the automatic
translation of foreign languages. The general Theory of
Communications asserts that noiseless exchange of accurate
information *is* the order, value, and meaning of the universe. And people feel that by language one can no longer
communicate anything.

But there is a meaning of "communication" by which
we say, "They seem to be talking the same language, but
they are not communicating"—that is, the speakers are
not referring to the same situation or are not taking it in
the same way; or even when they seem to agree, instead of
thereby having an identity of purpose with one another
and being able to cooperate, each continues in a parallel
course in isolation; their speech has made no difference to
them. Here, "communication" means that the speakers
touch one another. Their speech has made a difference to
how they organize their experience. A good sign of it is
that they thenceforth use their own words differently. The

essence is not the exchange of "information"; the information must form, re-form, the speakers. For this, the public constancy of the code is a disadvantage. To put it paradoxically, the aim of communication is to alter the code.

If I ask, "What time is it?" and you say, "Eight o'clock," and I go about my business using the information, my code is not deranged; I am set up for the information. Yet it is communication, because the information fills my need and makes a difference. But if I am surprised by what you say—I had counted on its being seven thirty and I am late—there is *more* communication! Your response has made *my* language more for real. In most conversation, however, the speakers interpret one another's remarks according to their own habits in order to *avoid* derangement; information is exchanged—e.g. the sentences can be repeated later—but it is reasonable to say there has been no communication. But in the closer contact of dialogue, as Buber calls it, there is resistance, vulnerability, reaching, excitement, and reconstruction. Since people's personalities are very much their verbal patterns, communication feels like physical aggression or seduction.

Poetic speech, which drastically alters the code, communicates better than ordinary speech; one has to give in to it to get something out of it. The non-verbal contact of persons, if it wrenches their expectations, is usually more communicative than any speech—consider a stealthy sexual touch, or a slap in the face. As I have said before, a chief purpose of the speech of psychotherapy is to change the language, especially the syntax.

But I think that this is also the idea of feedback in the usage of wise cyberneticists like Wiener or Gregory Bateson: The communicators impart novelty in the exchange of information; stereotypes convey little and just increase the noise; the more speech approximates to an exchange between identical filing cabinets, the less the communication. But then we must say that the code of the exchange is always being reconstructed in use by feedback, there are no fixed counters. And the speakers cannot finally be dissolved into bits of information, because as originators of novelty they are whole, free agents in the sense that they are outside the system being considered, whatever it is.

I disagree with Vygotsky:

Direct communication between minds is impossible, not only physically but psychologically. Thought must pass through meanings and these through words. . . . To understand another's speech, it is not sufficient to understand his words, we must understand his thought.

("Thought," we saw, was the internalized system of abstractions.) I rather agree with Merleau-Ponty that communication begins with people's bodies; this is by no means physically impossible. It is not minds that communicate, but people. The use of words is itself a creative act, somewhat physical, that produces meanings that did *not* exist in prior thought. People are more changed by changing their patterns of words than their thoughts. Good speech, colloquial or literary, is more meaningful than thought, not less, because it is part of a richer human situation, the dialogue of persons.

I realize that it is awkward and inelegant to define communication as I here propose; it is hard to build on it a precise Theory of Communications. It brings back the speakers and respondents as persons rather than exchangers of bits of information. If the speakers are free agents, we cannot know them through and through. What they do is probably not arbitrary, but *their* causes are outside the speech event and partly outside the realm of signs altogether. It is not possible to tell beforehand what sentences will be "meaningful" for communication. It is possible, even frequent, that it is some unnoticed nuance or connotation of the signs, or a fleeting gesture, even a "misunderstanding," that in fact communicates, rather than the common code or the prefabricated representations.

In this respect, a good conversation is like a unique artwork, unthinkable *a priori,* yet achieved, and then usually analyzable. It is only a literary or dramatic structural analysis of the actual speech event that can explain its functioning as communication.

7

The method of the linguist very much decides how "constant" the code is.

Like any other animal moving in a various and always somewhat novel field, a speaker must be able to say something new; coping with the environment, he will use neologism, metaphor, connotation, an exploratory word order. But to maintain his own equilibrium he must appropriate his new experience in a form traditional to himself, and he will favor the code, the dictionary meaning, denotation, formal word order. Thus, in linguistic research, if the speaker's response is restricted to his own judgment, as in the pair test or being asked what is grammatical, he will speak mostly code; but in spontaneous practical situations, he will speak with more variety and novelty.

Unless there is a fixed code, speaker and hearer cannot communicate; yet both speaking and hearing are active processes that shape speech for the occasion. If speech is too standard, it becomes an obstacle between speaker and hearer, like a foreign language; rather than speaking, the speakers have to translate. So in linguistic research, if language is isolated as an independent object of study, it will seem to be a constant code; but if we start from actual communication and ask what part language is playing in it, we will be struck by the flexibility of native speech. It will seem more a natural than a conventional behavior, more a creative adjustment than an algorithm or a pattern of culture.

The pattern of culture is itself ambiguous. A society determines the habits of its members; although there are always individual differences, the forces of imitation, co-operation, and conformity are overriding. But society is in more rapid flux than we usually judge. (Consider that the grandfather of a reader of this book might have conversed with George Washington.) If only because of unequal development during rapid change, most societies consist of a complex of small sub-societies. This and many other reasons make for intimate communities of speech. And also for much creole speech. Thus, it is not to express his individuality, but just to cooperate and conform, to form himself on a social model, that each speaker must continually alter the code he has learned. So in linguistic method, an instantaneous cut will reveal a constant code; but a more plausible historical stretch, that allows for sub-groups to impinge on one another, will show much more modification as the individuals adjust to one another and to their own changes.

Whether to assert or communicate or serve as a social bond, language must both be definite and have wide leeway. To be meaningful, it must also take the risk of being delusory or mere word-play.

CHAPTER XII

Notes for a Defence of Poetry

1 . Summary of This Book

Language is not a congenial scientific subject matter; it does not lend itself to a simple converging theory that explains what goes on. In order to make mathematical models, structural linguists disregard the influence of meaning, which is what the speakers are after. Theorists of Communications save the meanings, the patterns of information, but they tend to leave out the speakers and hearers, so that the theory of language becomes a branch of physics or physical biology. To get their fixed counters, positivists disregard the continual variation and invention in use. Anthropologists identify the language with the pattern of the culture, so that the universal human and animal functions of language that cross boundaries and change culture become inexplicable. In general, to make their simple theories work, all these rely on artifacts, like postulated expressions in ellipses or a constant code; or they use a method which freezes actual speech, like the pair test. But on the other hand, in order to affirm the freedom and meaning-making of language, phenomenologists disregard its conventionality and instrumentality; they stretch the meaning of "words" till the whole world is made of words.

By and large, older philologists did not come on as scientists or philosophers, but as naturalists, historians, and men of letters, and so they could allow the various aspects and uses of language to live and breathe together, with no systematic order. There would be chapters on the physiology of the speech organs, history and geography, etymology, semantical changes, syntax and comparative syntax, magic, logic, culture and literature, dialects and pidgins, artificial languages, etc. To bind it all together, they might use a convenient definition like "language is the chief means of conveying thought." The advantage of this definition was that, except for a few who were very psychology-minded (and fanciful), they did not bother with it further. And anyway, "thought" has as many various aspects and uses as language itself, so it imposes no order, sets no limits—and provides no explanations.

Colloquial speakers, of course, do not need to explain what they are doing when they speak their language. They use their inherited code and modify it. They try to be clear to the hearers, but they rely on them to make sense of what is being said. They use language to say propositions and to say nothing, to be sociable, to command, reveal, and deceive. They have their own style, they are culture-bound, they speak scientifically and with broad perspective. They use the words accurately as signs, and they get lost in words. They try to be correct, but they say their say any way they can. They adjust to dialects, they use language as a badge. They use language as a means for their ends, but their personalities and purposes are largely made of language. They speak complete sentences, shortened forms of complete sentences, redundancies beyond complete sentences, and forms that have not gotten to be complete sentences. They say the phonemes accurately; they miss the phonemes to a degree that should be confusing, but they are understood anyway; they use all kinds of "para-linguistic" noises as part of their language. They imitate like parrots, and they derive grammatical sentences which they have never heard. They communicate mostly speaking, mostly not speaking, and speaking and not speaking in combination. Finally, any of these may occur not in exceptional cases but with very many speakers in many situations. There is no good reason to exclude any of it as essentially not language. For special purposes, an investigator may abstract this or that use for concentrated study; but in my opinion he will make false statements about his abstracted part if he does not keep the rest in mind, as what speakers do when they speak language.

Instead, I have tried to stay with a few observations that are *prima facie*. Speakers speak to cope verbally with a situation when it is more appropriate (in their fallible judgment) than not speaking. The transaction of speaker and hearer is fundamental, though the hearer may not respond nor even, as in poetry, be a real person. For this transaction, the speakers use an inherited code (which could be called a "means"), but it is not constant, and the actual language is a tension between the code and what needs to be said. Communication is not the conveyance of meanings from one head to another by means of language; it is the language itself being said and understood. Finally, I have suggested that the wisest method of exploring language is to analyze how it operates in actual concrete situations, rather than deciding beforehand what "language" is. This is similar to the literary analysis of particular works; and, as in literary criticism, conversations and discourses fall roughly into genres, such as small talk, intimate talk, gang

talk, public exchange of information, talk of different
social classes, poems, journalism, dialogue, neurotic verbalizing, scientific exposition, etc. Each of these might
have, roughly, certain distinctive characteristics of pronunciation, grammar, lexicon, concreteness of denotation,
assertion of propositions, personal engagement of the
speakers, modifying of the standard code, tone of voice,
interplay of speaker and hearer, intermixture of the non-
verbal, order of exposition, etc. I may be mistaken, but I
think that a reasoned description of such genres would tell
us something about language that we have not been getting
from linguists, anthropologists, and philosophers.

2

Deliberate literature, oral or written, is not spontaneous speech, but it has compensating advantages in providing samples for exploring language. In the process of
making literature, an author finds his structure in handling
the words, and he does not exclude any aspect or use of
language—at any turn he may resort to precise denotation
or metaphor or syllogism or a dramatic colloquial scene,
or say his feelings. And he has to make the words fill out
what the ordinary speaker relies on non-verbal means to
do. There is no active respondent, so a literary work has to
incorporate both sides of the dialogue. This inevitably
produces a certain amount of idiolect—the writer's whim
or delusion of what English is or should be—yet writers are
also more than average respectful of the tradition and
genius of the language: They are its keepers. An artist
organizes a whole work, with beginning, middle, and end,
so it is usually possible to figure out what the various parts
are accomplishing—whether the choice of words, the syntax, the metaphor, the connotations, the tone and rhythm,

the narrative or dramatic manner. And of course a literary work is a concrete whole of speech that stands fixed, is repeatable, lets itself be examined closely.

In general, a stretch of good colloquial speech is a better example of the power of language than most writing. But there are thousands of literary works that are beyond comparison, just as there must be innumerable cases of excellent colloquial speech constantly occurring, apt and dramatic, beyond comparison. My bias is that we best catch the essence of a coping behavior like speech when it is operating at its best: Good literary works are good samples; excellent moments of common speech are even better samples, but they are elusive.

It has been argued, however, that the literary use of language is simply outmoded in modern times. It is neither the common speech that the anthropologists are after, and the linguists say they are after, nor is it the speech for good communication that the language reformers and the people in Communications are after. There is a famous analysis of the history of poetry and human speech that makes literature now quite irrelevant. On this view, poetry was the inevitable and appropriate speech of primitive ages, as the only available way of saying reality when not much was known and before the division of labor; these were ages of myth, when people living in a fearful and uncontrollable environment could not distinguish magic and science, nor saga and history, nor dream and empirical experience; the poets were the prophets, historians, philosophers, and scientists. In the course of time, poetry was replaced by philosophy and history; and these in turn have given way to special physical sciences and positivist sociology. In our time, literature can be merely decoration or entertainment or exercises in emotional noises. This was the line of Vico (on one interpretation) and of Comte. And prophylactic empiricist languages, like Basic English or positivist logic, carry it out as a program.

Apologists for literature have tended to regard exactly the same development of language as a devolution rather than an evolution. In his *Defence of Poesy* Philip Sidney argues that history and moral philosophy are ineffectual to teach the man of action and the warrior—he comes on strongly as the Renaissance scholar-poet who is also soldier-statesman. History tells us only what has been, poetry what should be; moral philosophy is dry analysis, poetry motivates to emulation and action. He would certainly not have been happier with the "value-neutral" language of present departments of sociology. In its high Italian form, Sidney's argument goes so far as to deny that scientific or philosophical sentences are true at all; only Eloquence is true, for truth resides in right action, not in propositions, just as Nietzsche holds that the only true science is the *Gaya Scienza* that makes you happy if you know it.

Shelley, in his *Defence of Poetry*, takes the same tack. He sees the world of his time as fragmented, quantified, rule-ridden; it is only poetry that can liberate and bring the parts together:

> The great secret of morals is love, or a going out of our own nature and an identification of ourselves with the beautiful which exists in thought, action, or person. . . . A man, to be greatly good, must imagine intensely and comprehensively. . . . Poetry enlarges the circumference of the imagination by replenishing it with thoughts of ever new delight, which have the power of attracting and assimilating to their own nature all other thoughts.
>
> We want the creative faculty to imagine that which we know: our calculations have outrun conception. . . . The cultivation of those sciences which have en-

larged the limits of the empire of man over the external
world has, for want of the poetrical faculty, propor-
tionately circumscribed those of the internal world. . . .
In my opinion, there is a lot of truth in this—it is grounded
in Coleridge's post-Kantian epistemology. It *is* odd, however, that as a philosophic anarchist after Godwin, Shelley
should end his *Defence* with the fatuous sentence, "Poets
are the unacknowledged legislators of the world." What
does he intend? That they should be acknowledged? Then
what would they do?

Depressed by the passing of Faith, Matthew Arnold—
in *Literature and Dogma, Culture and Anarchy,* and the
debate with Huxley—deplores the language of the church-
men, the Liberal and Radical economists, and the scientists, and he turns desperately to literature to give a standard for "Conduct" for the majority of mankind. Astound-
ingly, this view has condemned him as an élitist—in a
speech by Louis Kampf of M.I.T., the president of the
Modern Language Association! But Arnold is explicitly
drawing on the Wordsworthian doctrine that uncorrupted
common speech, heightened by passion and imagination,
binds mankind together, whereas the utilitarian speech of
the Liberals or the ideological speech of the Radicals destroys humanity. Professor Kampf singles out a passage of
Marx on the miserable education of poor children, to show
the virtues of a political radical who wants to change society. It is a fine humane passage. But I am sure the professor of English knows that it can be paralleled by, for
instance, Arnold's blistering attack in *Culture and Anarchy*
on the Philistine journalism of that same society for its
account of "the woman Smith" who had been arrested.
What is pathetic about Arnold, however, is his delusion,
shared by both Liberals and Radicals, that good speech
can somehow be learned in schools. Wordsworth did not
make this mistake.

Nearer to our own times, bureaucratic, urbanized, impersonalized, and depersonalized, Martin Buber could no longer rely even on literature, but went back to face-to-face dialogue, the orally transmitted legends of the Chasidim, and the psychotic experiences that underlie the text of the Bible. And we have seen that, in the present deep skepticism about specialist sciences and scientific technology, the young do not trust speech altogether, but only touching or silence.

In this dispute about the evolution of positivist language or the devolution to positivist language, both sides exaggerate (as usual). It is for quite reasonable human purposes that we have developed languages that are more accurately denotative and analytic and simpler in syntax than poetry. But the broader function of literary language, including poetry, also remains indispensable, because we are never exempt from having to cope with the world existentially, morally, and philosophically; and there is always emerging novelty that calls for imagination and poetry.

Consider the world-wide unease about the technology, the social engineering, the specialist sciences and their positivist value-neutral language. Suddenly, the line of dissent of Blake, Wordsworth, Shelley, William Morris, the symbolists, and the surrealists no longer seems to be the nostalgic romanticism of a vanishing minority, but the intense realism of a vanguard. I have found that I can mention even Jefferson and ruralism without being regarded as a crank. To try to cope with modern conditions by the methods of laboratory science, statistics, and positivist logic has come to seem obsessional, sometimes downright demented, as in the game strategies for nuclear warfare. As in a dream, people recall that technology is a branch of moral philosophy, with the forgotten criteria of prudence, temperance, amenity, practicality for ordinary use; and they ask for a science that is ecological and modestly naturalistic rather than aggressively experimental. But one cannot *do* moral philosophy, ecology, and naturalism without literary language. It was only a few years ago that C. P. Snow berated literary men for their ignorance of positive science, and now it is only too clear that there is an even greater need for positive scientists who are literary. Unfortunately, since men of letters have for so long let themselves be pushed out, we don't have relevant literary language and topics to say right technology and ecology; our usual literary attempts are apocalyptic, sentimental, out of date, or private.

A physician, for instance, is faced with agonizing dilemmas: euthanasia when novel techniques can keep tissue alive; birth control and the destiny of a person as a human animal; organ transplants and Lord knows what future developments; the allocation of scarce resources between the vital statistics of public health and the maximum of individual health, or mass practice and family practice. How does one spell out the Hippocratic oath in such issues? How can anyone by his own intuition and individual ratiocination, usually in crisis, possibly decide wisely and without anxiety and guilt? Yet there are almost no medical schools that find time for the philosophy of medicine. And we do not have the linguistic analysis, the reasoned description of precedents, the imagined situations, in brief the literature, for such philosophy.

The social sciences have been positivist only during my lifetime, though Comte talked it up a hundred fifty years ago. Marx was still able to say that Balzac was the greatest of the sociologists. Comte himself was energized by a crazy utopian poetry. Sir Henry Moore, Frederic Maitland, Max Weber, and so forth were historians, humanists. Geddes, Dewey, and Veblen were practical philosophers. Freud and Rank came on like a kind of novelists and fantasists and posed the problems for anthropology. It is, of course, a matter of opinion whether, after so many lisping centuries, the brief reign of mature sociology has been brilliant.[1] My hunch is that, despite a few more years guaranteed by big funding, it is moribund, done in by the social critics and the politically engaged of the past decades, who have had something useful to say. As one of the social critics, I can affirm that we are *philosophes,* men of letters.

Humanly speaking, the special sciences and their positivist language have been deeply ambiguous. At their best —it is a splendid best—they have gotten (and deserved) the pay-off of the theological virtues of faith, selflessness, and single-minded devotion, and of the moral virtues of honesty, daring, and accuracy. In Chapter VII, I singled out the operational language of Rudolf Carnap's *Testability and Meaning* as an exquisite vernacular. Such science is one of the humanities; its language is difficult because what it says is subtle and strange, minute in detail, sweepingly general. At their worst, however—and it is a very frequent worst—specialist science and its value-neutral language are an avoidance of experience, a narrow limitation of the self, and an act of bad faith. It is obsessional, an idolatry of the System of Science rather than a service to the unknown God and therefore to mankind. Needless to say, such science can be easily bought by money and power.

1. A recent study captained by Karl Deutsch, emanating from the University of Michigan, points to the great advances in recent years made by big teams of scholars heavily financed; and it refers sarcastically to those—namely me—who claim that we don't know much more than the ancients did about psychology, pedagogy, politics, or any other field where they had adequate empirical evidence. When I look at the list of great advances, however, I find them heavily weighted toward methodology and equipment: stochastic models, computer simulation, large-scale sampling, game theory, structural linguistics, cost-benefit analysis, etc., etc.—in brief, an enormous amount of agronomy and farm machinery and battalions of field-hands, but few edible potatoes.

Its language is boring because what the men do is not worth the effort, when it is not actually base. Being busy-work and form-ridden, it has no style.

3

I have written forty books. Evidently, to make literature is my way of being in the world, without which I would be at a loss. If I here examine and write the Apology for this behavior, I find that it is not very different from the older Defences of Poetry; but I do not need to make their exaggerated claims, since I am just describing my own situation. (Maybe it is simply that Sidney and Shelley were thirty years old, and I am sixty.)

I have a scientific disposition, in a naturalistic vein. I get a continual satisfaction from seeing, objectively, how things are and work—it makes me smile, sometimes rue-fully—and I like to write it down. But I do not exclude how I am and work as one of the things, unfortunately an omnipresent one in my experience. (I can occasionally smile at this too, but I am happier when I am not there.) God is history—how events actually turn out—but history includes also the history of me. God creates the world and I am only a creature, but I *am* a creature and He takes me into account, though He doesn't always know what's good for me and I complain a lot. Thus, my objective natural-istic sentences are inevitably colored by, and likely dis-torted by, my own story and feelings. They turn into literature.

I cannot take my wishes, feelings, and needs for granted and directly try to act them, as many other people seem to be able. I have to try to make sense—that is, to say my feelings and needs to myself and to other people. It is no doubt the sign of a deep anxiety; I cannot manage the

callousness of healthy good conscience, though I do not
feel much conscious guilt. I have to justify my needs with
meanings. Conversely, I try to translate into action the
meanings that I say, for, as with everybody else, much of
the meaning that I know is unsatisfactory and something
should be done about it. The combination of action and
meaning also results in a lot of literature, rhetoric, social
criticism, psychoanalysis, pedagogy, and press conferences.

Whether by nature or long habit that has become second nature, I have that kind of personality that first says
and then initiates what it wants, and then knows what it
wants, and then wants it. Before saying, I feel just a vague
unrest. With most people, it is wise to take seriously what
they do, not what they say; their words are rationalizations,
pious platitudes, or plain hypocrisy. But writers' words
commit them, marshal their feelings, put them on the spot.
I make a political analysis because I have a spontaneous
gift for making sense; I then have to go through with the
corresponding political exercise, unwillingly not because
I am timid but because I am lousy at it. I tentatively say
"I love you" and find that I love you. Or very often I have
said what seems to me to be a bluff, beyond what I know
or want, and it proves to be after all what I mean. Like
the Egyptian god that Otto Rank mentions, a writer makes
himself by saying.

I am in exile. Like everybody else, I live in a world
that is given to me—I am thankful for it. It is not made
by me—and that too is very well. But it is *not* my native
home; therefore I make poems. "To fashion in our lovely
English tongue a somewhat livelier world, I am writing
this book" (*The Empire City*). In order to appropriate this
unfeeling bitter place where I am a second-class citizen.
I was no happier when I was young, and I wrote poems;
it is no bed of roses when I am toothless and have failing
eyes, and I write poems. I never was a beauty, to get what

I wanted sexually, but now I am also too tired to seek for it. But even worse than my private trouble is how men have made of the earth an object of disgust, and the stupidity and pettiness of statesmen tormenting mankind and putting additional obstacles in the way, as if life were not hard enough. It does not help, either, that people are so pathetic, the apparently powerful as much as the powerless. To pity is another drain of spirit. But it helps me to say it just as it is, however it is.

Also, I am good at thinking up little expedients of how it could be otherwise. I tend not to criticize, nor even to notice, until I can imagine something that would make more sense. My expedients are probably not workable in the form I conceive them, and I certainly do not know how to get them adopted—they are utopian literature—but they rescue me from the horror of metaphysical necessity, and I hope they are useful for my readers in the same way. When they are neat solutions, they make a happy comic kind of poetry. Maybe they are all the more charming because they are practical, simple-minded, and impossible. It is the use of comic writing.

Meaning and confusion are both beautiful. What is chilling is great deeds that have no meaning—the stock in trade of warriors and statesmen, but my radical friends also go in for them. What is exasperating is positivistic clarity and precision that are irrelevant to the real irk. A value of literature is that it can inject confusion into positivistic clarity, bring the shadows into the foreground.

Ancient and modern writers are my closest friends, with whom I am in sympathy. They are wise and talented and their conversation sends me. Maybe I am lonely more than average (How would I know?), but I need them. Books and artworks are extraordinary company (one does not need to make allowances), and in the nature of the case, they speak most clearly to us writers and artists because we respond to them most actively; we notice how he does that, and if it is congenial we say, "I could do something like that." Despite its bloodlessness, the tradition of litera-ture is a grand community and, much as I envy the happy and the young, I doubt that they have as good a one. (How would I know?) Freud said that artists, giving up animal satisfaction and worldly success for their creative life, hope by this detour to win money, fame, and the love of women. He was wrong; I never had such a hope, but I have thereby entered a company that has given me many beautiful hours. Often, talking to young people at their colleges, when I quote from great writers whom I evidently treat as familiars, they look at me with envy because I have a tradition which they lack, through no fault of theirs, but I do not know how to pass it on.

And what a thing it is to write English sentences! rapid in thought, sometimes blunt sometimes sinuous in syntax. Underlying my gripe in this book against the anthropol-ogists and the linguists is simply that they do not love my language and have done nothing for it; whereas one of the reasons I am partial to Otto Jespersen is that he loved English and praised it and cast light on it, though he wrote it indifferently (it was not his mother tongue).

I showed some of these chapters in typescript to Ivan Illich in Cuernavaca. He said to me gloomily that *he* had no native tongue. He speaks many languages fluently, but the chances of his life have been such that he cannot think or write his own language (I don't know whether it was Serbian or Croatian). It was perceptive of him to hear that my chief message is that I love American English. She has loved me.

When writing, I take my syntax and words from my colloquial speech; I strongly disapprove of the usual dis-tinction between "standard colloquial" and "standard lit-erary." I will write the slang that I consider worth using when I talk, for instance in the last few pages I have written "he comes on as," "their conversation sends me," "Comte talked it up," "they have gotten the pay-off," "it is for real." I like the texture woven of the rough and slangy, the learned and periodic, and the oddly accurate; it says "me," a scholar in poor clothes with a sharp mind. I have no doubt that my voice can be heard in my writing by those who know me face-to-face. Lecturing, I just muse along and think aloud in a conversational tone, referring to a few notes I have jotted down. When I read verse aloud, I again use a conversational tone and follow the on-going prose sense rather than the sonority, meter, imagery, or drama. I do not try to be portentous:

> Say my song simply for its prosy sentence,
> cutting at the commas, pausing at the periods.
>
> Any poetry in it will then be apparent,
> motion of mind in English syntax.

On the other hand, though I follow the sense, I am *not* intent on conveying any truth or message, but just the beginning, middle, and end of a whole literary work. I will strike whatever impedes or detracts from the whole, regardless of the "truth." For what I communicate must, in the end, be not anything I know but how I do in getting *rid* of the poem, putting it out there. Afterwards, God help me, I am left so much the less.

I use the word "God" freely when I write, much less freely when I speak, never when I think or talk to myself. I don't know clearly what I intend by it. I cannot pray in any usual sense, though I sometimes use the awareness exercises of psychotherapy which, I guess, is my religion. But in writing of the fundamental relations of my soul, mankind, and the world, I find the terminology of St. Thomas or Karl Barth far more congenial and accurate than that of Freud or Wilhelm Reich, who are either too "subjective" or too "objective"; they do not say how it is. To say deliberately just how it is with me is apparently how I pray, if I may judge by the language that comes to me—especially when I am at a loss for grief, confusion, gratitude, or fear. In moments of impasse—but only when I have earned the right to say it because I have tried hard— I have written "Creator spirit, come."

Maybe it is that when I think or talk to myself, I am embarrassed, but when I write I am not embarrassed. I now remember that I fell on my knees and said a prayer when I had *finished* writing *The Empire City,* and indeed the ending of that book is very good.

When I write public themes—urbanism, psychology, delinquency, the school system, the use of technology, re-sisting the draft—I of course try to be honest with the facts, to "save the phenomena," but again I rather obviously put more trust in the literary process, the flow of saying my say, than in statistics. I take the statistics seriously when they contradict me; I modify my line or make a distinction, or I explain how the statistics are an artifact or haven't asked the right question. I like using abrasive material to work with, and I have no impulse to sweep difficulties under the rug. (Sometimes, however, I am simply ignorant.) But when the "facts" run positively in my direction, I do not argue from them but treat them literarily: 85 percent becomes "a good majority," 60 percent is "in very many cases," 35 percent is "an appreciable number of cases," 20 percent is "sometimes it happens that." A single indi-vidual whom I judge to be typical, and where I can pro-vide a global, literary, explanation to my satisfaction, weighs more than all the rest, because he is for real and must be coped with politically and humanly. Except for rhetorical effect, I usually don't make generalizations any-way, because I don't care about them—when I do make them they tend to be outrageous because I am outraged.

I do not understand a cause or a reason as a correlation, but animally, as continuous with a muscular push or a perceptual Gestalt.

But when I rely on the literary process, the flow of saying my say, this does not mean that I say what I *want* to say but what *can*—strongly—be said. The work has its own discipline, to be clear, to make sense, to hang together, to go from the beginning to the end. For instance, I do not allow myself the usual concessive clause "although some cases are not so-and-so, yet the majority of cases are so-and-so." Such a construction is stylistically feeble. If there are well-marked exceptions or a single outstanding exception, it is better to find the distinction that explains the exception and to *affirm* it rather than concede it. The difference will then strengthen the explanation of the other cases; it will provide a new reason. Often it provides the best reason, the one I hadn't thought of till I had to write the sentence. A strong and scrupulous style is a method of discovery.

Commenting on this, an unfriendly critic night say, "You mean that it is true if it sounds good." To which I would reply, in an unfriendly tone of voice, "Yes."

My reliance on colloquial speech and the process of literature is certainly closely related, whether as cause or effect, to my political disposition. I am anarchistic and agitational, and I am conservative and traditional. So is good speech. Insistently and consistently applied, any humane value, such as common sense, honor, honesty, humor, or compassion, will soon take one far out of sight of the world as it is; and to have meaning is one of the virtues that is totally disruptive of established institutions. Nevertheless, meaningful language and coherent syntax are always historical and traditional and always have a kind of logic. Speaking is a spontaneous action of the speaker, and he speaks only in a community, for a hearer. Colloquial speech cannot be regimented, whereas even perception and science can be regimented—perception because it is solitary and passive, science because they can put blinders on it like a directed horse. But the vulnerability of colloquial, we saw, is that its freedom is limited to where the speakers have initiative, eye-witnessing, and trust, and these limits may be made narrow indeed. But the literary process expands these limits by historical memory, international culture, and welcoming the dark unconscious which common folk prudently inhibit. Common speech can be pretty empty and aimless, whereas to write you must know at least something and try to be clear—it is a profession.

Slogans can't last long in either common speech or literature. In agitated situations, the new people, making bad literature (and sometimes even writing it down), always recall ancient languages, as the Reformers picked up the Hebrew patriarchs, the French Revolutionists picked up Marcus Brutus, the radical students pick up Marx, and the Hippies pick up various Indians and Amerindians; but the good writers ridicule these too.

Thus, my Apology for the literature to which I have given the years of my life is very like other Defences of Poetry over several centuries. It is noteworthy that they are all similar. Possibly if we had different communities, we would say something different; but possibly it is the human condition. (How would I know?) Literature confounds personal and impersonal, meaning and beginning to act, thought and feeling. In this confusion, which is like actual experience, it makes a kind of sense. It imagines what might be, taking account of what is. Using the code of language, it continually revises the code to cope with something new. It is more conservative than science and more daring than science. It makes the assured and powerful uneasy, if only out of powerless spite. It speaks my common speech and it makes human speech noble. It

provides me a friendly community across ages and boundaries and cheers my solitude. I join in. Writing is not
boring. It is the way I pray to God and my present community. As a writer I am patriotic—democratic—legiti-
mate as the royal family—and to be meaningful, I rebel.

About
the Author

Paul Goodman, a native New Yorker, was born in 1911.
After graduating from City College in New York, he
received his Ph.D. in humanities from the University of
Chicago. Mr. Goodman has taught at the University
of Chicago, New York University, Black Mountain
College, Sarah Lawrence, the University of Wisconsin, and
the University of Hawaii, and has lectured at three
hundred universities throughout the country.

He is an associate of the Institute for Policy Studies
in Washington and the Institute for Gestalt Therapy
in New York.

Mr. Goodman is one of the most well-known literary
and social critics of our time. His articles have appeared
in *Commentary, The New York Review of Books,
Politics, Kenyon Review, Resistance, Liberation,
Partisan Review,* and other periodicals. Vintage Books
has reprinted several of Mr. Goodman's well-known
longer works of social criticism, among them *Growing
Up Absurd, Utopian Essays and Practical Proposals,
The Community of Scholars* and *Compulsory
Mis-education* (both in one volume), *People or Personnel*
and *Like a Conquered Province* (also combined in
one volume), and *Five Years.* His most recent work
of social criticism is *New Reformation: Notes of
a Neolithic Conservative.*

He is also the author of *Three Plays: The Young
Disciple, Faustina, and Jonah.* He has published three
volumes of verse—*Homespun of Oatmeal Gray, Hawkweed,*
(both available in Vintage books), and *The Lordly Hudson*
—and collected short stories, *Adam and His Works.*

Mr. Goodman's novels include *Parents' Day, The Empire
City,* and *Making Do. Kafka's Prayer* and *The Structure
of Literature* are books of literary criticism.

Paul Goodman is married, has two children, and lives
in New York City and New Hampshire.